KATHMANDU

Valley of the Green-Eyed Yellow Idol

KATHMANDU
Valley of the Green-Eyed Yellow Idol

by
Bob Gibbons & Siân Pritchard-Jones

PILGRIMS PUBLISHING
◆ Varanasi ◆

KATHMANDU: Valley of the Green-Eyed Yellow Idol
Bob Gibbons & Siân Pritchard-Jones

Published by:
PILGRIMS PUBLISHING

An imprint of:
PILGRIMS BOOK HOUSE
(Distributors in India)
B 27/98 A-8, Nawabganj Road
Durga Kund, Varanasi-221010, India
Tel: 91-542-2314060, 2312456
E-mail: pilgrims@satyam.net.in
Website: www.pilgrimsbooks.com

PILGRIMS BOOK HOUSE (New Delhi)
9 Netaji Subhash Marg, 2nd Floor
Near Neeru Hotel, Daryaganj
New Delhi 110002
Tel: 91-11-23285081
E-mail: pilgrim@del2.vsnl.net.in

Distributed in Nepal by:
PILGRIMS BOOK HOUSE
P O Box 3872, Thamel,
Kathmandu, Nepal
Tel: 977-1-4700942
Off: 977-1-4700919
Fax: 977-1-4700943
E-mail: pilgrims@wlink.com.np

Cover Art and Illustrations: Bob Gibbons
Colour Photos © SPJ and Bob Gibbons
Layout by Asha Mishra

ISBN: 81-7769-221-6

Printed in India at Pilgrim Press Pvt. Ltd. Lalpur Varanasi

CONTENTS

ABOUT THE AUTHORS

Bob Gibbons and Siân Pritchard-Jones have been visiting Nepal since 1974 and 1982 respectively. They have returned each year, usually to lead treks or to drive overland tours across India or Asia.

For some years now they have been helping with the editing and production of out-of-print books and other volumes for Pilgrims Publications in Kathmandu. Their first venture with Pilgrims was the publication of a trekking guide to Mustang and one to Tibet, also translated into French. Since then they have also written a trekking guide to the Everest region, with added cultural interest.

More recently they have broadened their knowledge considerably, with the research, collating and publication of the Erotic Art of the Kathmandu Valley and the introductory guides to Ayurveda and Vaastu, the ancient Indian art of building, as well as this guide to the Kathmandu Valley and a guide to Boudhanath.

They have also travelled extensively in and across Africa, and have written the fourth edition of the Bradt travel guide Africa by Road.

ACKNOWLEDGEMENTS

Thanks to Rama Tiwari for choosing us to write his erotic series and, in turn, inspiring us to get out and discover all the hidden corners of the valley. The ever-patient staff of Pilgrims, who have helped us to seek out the necessary information among the crowded bookshelves of the shop, deserve our thanks too.

Mr. Janaki Man Shrestha of J. B. Art Centre, Thahity Tole, helped us to identify the various bodhisattvas and allowed us the use of a golden Yab-Yum model for photography.

Chapter Four about the people of the valley was collated and written with the assistance of Naresh Subha, previously of Pilgrims Book House.

Thanks also to Mr. Karna Sakya and Mr. Sohan Shrestha of Kathmandu Guest House for their reminiscences, Mr. Yogendra and Mrs. Bindu Sakya of ACE Hotels for their hospitality in Nagarkot, Mr. K.C., founder of K.C.'s Restaurant for his stories, and Rum Doodle restaurant for their hospitality over the years.

And of course to Bhandari's Photo Shop in Thamel for their prompt and efficient service.

PREFACE

Welcome to Pilgrims new cultural guide to the Kathmandu Valley. This book is more than just a guide, for it includes anecdotes and memories of our experiences in the valley since 1974.

The Kathmandu Valley has perhaps the greatest concentration of temples, shrines and idols devoted to religion and traditions than anywhere in the world. This book is a journey back in time and around the delights of the valley.

A new day dawns with the glowing tinge of a Himalayan sunrise. Pilgrims pay homage to their gods; people bring offerings and venerate the deities. Smoke rises from incense sticks, butter lamps flicker in front of a golden image. Idols sit serene, posing for a thousand years in meditation. A bird circles and flies to the branches of a gigantic Banyan tree. Prayer flags flutter in unison with the chants of monks, a haunting sound of mesmerising charm.

These are the visions of a Kathmandu once calm, quiet and rural. That is a place that is hard to find today, with ever-increasing pressures of development and the urban population explosion. But it is still there; it takes time to find, but at any time one may stumble upon a place of beauty. A moment in time captures a distant image.

There are many aspects to the Kathmandu Valley. Its timeless history is buried in legends. Legends abound, tales, myths and folk stories are the lifeblood of its festivals. The gods, goddesses and deities are its backbone, upon whose shoulders its religion takes place. The art of the valley is intriguing. What secret notions are behind the amazing displays of erotic talent? Did one ever see such fanciful depictions anywhere else? And how do these imaginative creations intertwine with the beliefs in the valley?

The religious mingling of Hinduism, Buddhism, Tantra, Vajrayana, Tibetan sorcery and Shamanism is a mystery in itself.

We take you into the great Durbar Squares of the Malla Kings and explore dark narrow lanes to find strange idols. We follow the holy men to Pashupatinath. We join the Tibetans, Sherpa and Buddhist pilgrims circling the great stupas at Boudhanath and Swayambhu. In a quiet street of Bhaktapur, time stands still. Its mediaeval atmosphere is a living relic of a forgotten era. We also explore the lesser known shrines and temples, rarely noted by most guides. Places of surprising antiquity and often found in rural hidden corners.

Come with us around the valley to discover the fabulous architecture, the quaint delights, the strange idols, the overwhelming colours, the whimsical images and the enlightening vistas. All are to be found here beneath the never-ending gaze of the all-seeing eyes.

Bob Gibbons
Siân Pritchard-Jones
Kathmandu 2004

Authors' note: -

We apologise for any factual errors within the text. With so many different local interpretations of the culture we have seen, it is hard to discern the truth, if indeed any truth exists, among the legends and tales passed down over generations. Therefore it is likely that some explanations may vary, according to the source from which they came.

Please do let us know if you discover any more hidden gems within the valley which we should include in future editions.

—The Supreme Being is
thousand-headed,

Thousand-eyed, thousand-
footed;

He pervades the Universe on
all sides,

And extends beyond the ten
directions.

Rig-Veda. 10.90.1

Chaturmukha Lingam

CHAPTER ONE
Introduction

In the beginning was the Adi Buddha, the self-created, self-existent one known as Swayambhunath. And this Buddha, with curious mysterious eyes, came to reside on a hill that grew from the lotus plant out of a vast lake. And when the waters receded, the rich and pleasant valley became an enchanting garden, the garden of the Buddha, a valley of gods and goddesses, the valley of Kathmandu.

Kathmandu sits on the edge of the world, a lost paradise, a valley of hidden enchantment. It is a place as mysterious as the green-eyed yellow god. And where is this idol who keeps vigil over the valley; will we find it here below the Himalayas, the abode of the gods?

In exploring the Kathmandu Valley of Nepal, we take you on a magical tour of its myriad of sights. We travel back in time, to discover in brief some of the history of the valley. We meet the local people, introduce the different forms of religion, and explain the gods and goddesses. Then there are the festivals that influence the rich tapestry and heritage of the Kathmandu Valley. Along the way we pause to reminisce about times now past.

The Kathmandu Valley, located at an altitude of 1300 m (4200 ft), is a crossroads, a trading centre; a melting pot of migrating peoples and ideas. Before the first road was built over the Mahabharat ranges it took two long hard days of walking to reach the valley. Since the times of the earliest records, vague inscriptions on ancient pillars believed to date from the Ashokan period, the valley has had a mystical quality that has attracted much thought and worship. Great sages, philosophers, preachers and holy men have passed this way. This enchantment can still be discovered, but it is less evident today. Until the early 1980s, the valley was predominantly rural in character; one could hear the birds, see the mountains and breathe the fresh air. It was no false statement to say that the valley was enchanting; idols outnumbered people, and temples and pagodas, often over-grown and in a frightening state of collapse, outnumbered tourists.

Today all aspects of life can be found on the streets of the Kathmandu Valley. At night only the dogs disturb the silence, but as the dawn breaks, the villages and the city spring into life. People stir from their beds to answer the call of nature. Metal shutters rattle loudly as the shops open for yet another day of business in the city.

Gradually the cacophony and chaos on the roads builds up. Pedestrians, bicycles, cycle rickshaws, motorbikes, motor rickshaws, taxis, buses, trucks; all compete for space on the narrow lanes, highways and by-ways alike. But it's still possible to find quiet comers where little has changed for centuries. Beneath the intricately carved wooden temples, a man sits deep in thought; another reads the daily news, while another admires his reflection and the result of his recent visit to the barber's shop.

All ages enjoy just sitting talking, or simply thinking, for the pace of life is slow even in the capital of this Himalayan kingdom. Potters still spin their wares by hand on the streets; antique sewing machines perform miracles on antiquated clothing as well as modern fabrics. Tibetans spin their prayer wheels as they walk, sending their prayers for peace skywards. An old woman says "Namaste," with her hands together in the time-honoured gesture symbolising unity and love.

And the dogs lie quietly, in preparation for another night of action on the streets...

In some ways little has changed, but at least reaching the capital is now somewhat easier.

Nepal, Land of Mystery: **Hassoldt Davis 1939**

"The last stretch of the trail was a continuous zigzag of slime and rocks that came rushing upon us whenever we touched them. I crept on all fours, remembering too vividly the poor pilgrim who had catapulted down to death. I embraced the trees like brothers, and passed from trunk to trunk. Ten feet gained. Twenty-five. The ground was flattening and I could almost walk erect unaided. Then I suddenly reached level earth and saw the mountains slope down in front of me, the Chandragiri Pass. I stared. There below lay the valley of Nepal, legendary Kathmandu. Fog filled it. There lay the last home of mystery, a perfect blank."

Old Kathmandu

Buddha at Swayambhunath

CHAPTER TWO
The Historical Perspective

Once upon a time the Kathmandu Valley was a lake surrounded by forests and mountains. And deep in this lake lived the nagas, the mythical serpents or snakes. One day a wise sage, a messenger of the Buddha to come, climbed the hill known as Nagarjun and threw a lotus seed into the lake. After thousands of years, the seed blossomed and a lotus grew with thousands of petals and flowers. A great light issued forth from the centre of the great lotus plant.

Sometime after, Manjushri, a demon-like deity of the Buddha, passed by and, with a single blow of his sword, he cut a great gash in the hillside to the south. The water drained away, leaving a magnificent valley for the people to inhabit. And the great light shone forth until a priest came by and, realising a dark age was coming, hid the light under a precious stone. On this spot he built the great stupa now known as Swayambhunath. And the lotus plant flowed away and came to rest at a place now known as Pashupatinath.

But we digress, for this is the ancient legend about the birth of the Kathmandu Valley and it pre-dates the chronicled history of the valley.

Little is recorded about the original inhabitants of the valley, but they were known as the Kiranti people, who may have come from the eastern hilly districts. It was Ashoka (3rd century BC) who was widely credited with being one of the first emissaries of Buddhism in India and Nepal. The ancient stupas of Patan and a pillar in Lumbini are believed to have been built at that time. Ashoka followed the Buddha, Prince Siddhartha himself, who was born in Lumbini in southern Nepal, near the modern-day town of Bhairahawa. The Buddha travelled much in northern India, where his ideas took root.

Trade flourished; yak tails, copper and iron were all exchanged in these early years.

The Licchavi Period

More authenticated historical facts about the valley relate to the time of around 300 AD. Contacts between Nepal and India cemented the establishment of the Licchavi dynasty, which migrated from the city of Vaishali in northern India. With them came the Hindu traditions, the caste system, worship of the cow and other religious ideas. The kingdom of Vaishali extended north into modern-day Nepal, into the areas adjacent to Janakpur in the Terai. Remnants of the art forms of Vaishali, known as Mithila arts and crafts, are still found today in this region.

A Licchavi princess, Kumaradevi, married one of the Gupta kings who ruled India, and part of Nepal became a border state of the Indian Kingdom. Later on trade routes developed between Tibet and India, with Kathmandu being the most important link. On a pillar in the precincts of Changu Narayan temple, to the east of the city, an ancient inscription details some of the earliest recorded written knowledge of the valley.

The decline of Buddhism in India in the face of Hinduism corrupted the Buddhist ideals. Tantric ideas, which involved magical elements and physical methods of approaching Nirvana, led to a general liberalising and changing of Buddhist ideals. These ideas were later taken across the Himalayas and developed in Tibet. Here they became mixed with the indigenous animistic ideas of Bonpo, which prevailed in Tibet. The Tibetan King Srongtsen Gampo converted much of Tibet to Buddhism around 640 AD; he took both a Chinese and a Nepalese wife, who was called Princess Bhrikuti (one of the Taras depicted on Nepalese tangkas, religious paintings). Links between Tibet and Nepal strengthened during this period.

Padma Sambhava was another disciple of the Buddha; he travelled in the 8th century and later became worshipped as Guru Rinpoche. His knowledge of Tantra enabled him to subdue the demons and gods in Tibet. His miraculous powers came from the dakinis, demonic female deities.

Tibetan Buddhism still incorporates many animistic or shamanistic concepts, and this is often manifested in the gruesome-looking statues of the gods and bodhisattvas displayed in the monasteries. This form of Buddhism is prevalent in the mountain regions, where monasteries and their lamas still exhibit these traits and traditions.

The Malla Period

The earliest construction of multi-tiered palaces and pagodas probably occurred at this time. The people lived in decorated houses, using copper, and both Hindu and Buddhist shrines existed side by side. The end of the 8th century witnessed the end of the successful and prosperous Licchavi period. Few records exist of the period following the demise of the Licchavi until the 13th century, when the Malla Kings assumed power.

The only Muslim raids on the valley occurred in 1349, when the Bengali Sultan Sham Udin Ilyas attacked the cities and destroyed the Pashupati Lingam. It was rebuilt in1360.

Jayasthiti Malla, a Hindu, gained power when he married a princess of Bhaktapur, one of the small city states within the valley. By 1382, he had gained power over the Kathmandu Valley. He also declared himself to be a reincarnate of the god Vishnu, a practice that is still considered appropriate for the monarchs of Nepal. Law and order was established; the caste system was further developed. The Guthi, or local council, idea was strengthened and still exists today in the Newari communities that form the main ethnic group in the valley.

In the reigns of Jyoti Malla and Yaksha Malla things improved, with the kingdom expanding beyond the valley. After the death of Yaksha Malla around 1482, the three towns of Kathmandu, Patan and Bhaktapur became the city state capitals once again. Each king competed to build the greatest Durbar Square, the basis of those that exist today. Many of the festivals seen today were revived in this period of great architecture, art and culture. Trade with Tibet formed the basis of this wealth and prosperity.

Malla King on Pedestal

7

The Shah Kings

In the central mountains of Nepal, below the massive Himalayan peaks of Himalchuli and Baudha, lies the town of Gorkha. From a hilltop fortress, which still exists today with its quaint Durbar and stunning location, came Prithvi Narayan Shah, the ancestor of today's king. They swept in from the west, with armies to subdue and eventually control the valley and its three main cities. The smaller city of Kirtipur was the first to fall to Prithvi Narayan Shah, who became ruler of all Nepal and united the country as one. The year of his success was 1768. The last Malla King retreated to Bhaktapur, and with his death came the end of that glorious period of culture and art.

Nepalese armies invaded Tibet in 1788, but were later repulsed with Chinese intervention, and after this Nepal paid tribute to Tibet. However, the Gurkha armies controlled the land as far east as Sikkim, and west into Kumaon. In 1816 the British defeated the Gurkhas and, in the treaty of Segauli, Nepal had to cede Sikkim to India, with the borders established as they are now, along the Mahakali River in the west and the Mechi River in the east. The British established a resident office, but Nepal effectively became a closed land after 1816.

The Ranas

In 1846 a soldier of the court by the name of Jung Bahadur Kunwar Rana took power after a bloody massacre in the Kot Square adjacent to the Kathmandu Durbar Square. Jung Bahadur Rana was a deceptive inter-loper who, through various court intrigues, ingratiated himself with the Queen. After the murder of a high official, the Queen assembled her minis-ters at the Kot Square to find the perpetrator of the crime. In the Kot massacre most of the nobles, courtiers and minister died. The Queen was sent into exile and the King dethroned.

For the next hundred years Nepal was ruled by the Rana family, who called themselves Maharajas to distinguish them from the Shah Kings, who were all but powerless. The Ranas intermarried with the Shah off-spring, but were not at all effective rulers. Family intrigues, murder and treachery dominated the activities as much as the job of administering the country. The Ranas built some magnificent palaces after one of them vis-ited England; many of these buildings still exist today, but they are mostly in a sorry state of disrepair. The country remained closed to all but a few

8

invited guests and, as a result, retained its medieval traditions and beliefs until the mid 20th century.

The Martyrs for Democracy

After Indian independence in 1947, a Congress Party was formed in Kathmandu. The powerless King became a symbol for freedom from the Ranas' autocratic rule.

At the time of the Ranas, it was a crime for the ordinary people of the country to show any sign of wealth or prosperity. One businessman who returned from India in a carriage drawn by four horses was badly beaten for his "sins". Education for the common people was also regarded as a crime. Teachers lived and taught in fear of their lives. In the struggle for freedom and human dignity, an organisation called Nepal Praja Parishad was formed, demanding respect and freedom for all the people.

But for those who dared to confront the Ranas, there was a terrible price to pay. Many young men in the prime of their lives faced the death penalty, and were either hanged from trees or taken to the riverbanks and shot.

On October 18th 1940, the poet Siddhi Charan Shrestha was returning home from his early morning walk at 7 a.m., six or seven soldiers approached him and said they were taking him in for interrogation. In his house, they searched through all the family papers, distressing his two-year-old son, pregnant wife and his parents. One month later his father was also taken and imprisoned in the old school building at Singha Durbar. Sadly they were never to meet again, and the son was not even allowed to carry out his father's funeral rites, which are so important to Hindus.

It was not until five years later that he was released, but not before many of his friends had been executed for opposing the Ranas. The first two to die were Shukra Raj, who was hanged on 23 January 1941, and Dharma Bhakta, who taught gymnastics to King Tribhuvan, but was hanged on 25 January 1941. A few days later two more young men, Gangalal and Dashrath Chand, were taken and shot at the confluence of the rivers Vishnumati and Bhacha Kola.

Dashrath Chand was a Thakuri, a caste close to the Ranas, and indeed he could have married one, as the Ranas often married their children to Thakuris. One of the Rana girls, Zulfia Maiya, fell in love with him, but such was his devotion to the country and the people that he refused to do so, knowing that he would have to dedicate his life to the struggle for democracy.

Ganesh Man Singh (1916-1998) was also imprisoned at this time, but he managed a miraculous escape with the use of a hook and a length of knotted cloth. He went on to become Supreme Leader of the Nepali Congress Party, and was still a significant figure at the time of the next revolution for democracy in 1990 under King Birendra.

In 1950 Tibet was invaded by China; refugees poured across the borders and by now the Ranas were unpopular and ineffective.

Return of the Shah Kings

After a decade of suffering and horrific human rights abuses, a country-wide rebellion, supported by King Tribhuvan, finally removed the Ranas in 1951. With assistance from India and the forces for democracy, King Tribhuvan assumed power. A coalition government was installed, with some form of democracy. The country opened its borders to outsiders, and Mount Everest was climbed in May 1953. King Tribhuvan died in 1955 and his son Mahendra assumed power. In 1960 Mahendra declared a state of emergency and the brief experiment with democracy was closed. The King introduced the partyless panchayat system, which was based on local councils of elders with a tiered system up to the central parliament.

In 1972 King Birendra was installed as the new king. His coronation took place in 1975, when an auspicious date had been fixed.

In 1980 a referendum was held to decide between a continuing panchayat system or a political party-style democracy. The result was very close, but the panchayat system was retained. After 1985, rapid expansion brought many changes; the population grew by astonishing numbers. The old rural lifestyle of the valley began to disappear under a wave of construction. The panchayat system was preferred, but was softened, with some forms of elections permitted. With an increasing population, social poverty, corruption and mounting trade disagreements with India, demands for democracy grew.

April 1975—The Coronation

We head out from the Hotel Withes for Durbar Square along the empty lanes. Everyone is elsewhere today. Even the Swiss café is closed; only pigs and chickens scurry about the deserted streets. A solitary beggar woman sits on the steps of a temple, smoking a bidi.

From New Road the pageant begins; elephants enter the square, with bright red satin and golden brocade covering their bristling great bodies. Each rumbles past. The elephant driver, the mahout, edges his beast forward, his feet behind the ears controlling the elephant. The sky is a dazzling blue and above all this is the Hanuman Dhoka Palace, its towering pagodas casting a fantastic fairytale castle-like shadow. Bands of Gurkhas follow. Then come men in their finest traditional clothes. Horsemen and soldiers escort the procession. The crowd is ordered but animated. The hippies have been swept out of town.

This is a joyous day for all Nepal. The new King is crowned today.

Constitutional Monarchy

In April 1990 full-scale rioting and demonstrations broke out, eventually forcing the king to allow a democratic system to be implemented. Freedom of speech and press followed, and things took a turn for the better. The king remained as constitutional head, but in a mainly ceremonial position. Political corruption and infighting did little to enhance the democratic ideals, and in the late nineties a grass roots Maoist rebellion broke out. Many had sympathy with the need for greater social equality, but violence and demands for a leftist dictatorship met with resistance.

King's Plume

April 1990 Bob's story

All scheduled international flights are cancelled. For three days now we have been confined to the hotel most of the time. A curfew is in place and this is only lifted for an hour or so per day to allow people and tourists to go out and get food and water. At the Kathmandu Guest House, the only food is served in the evening. The guests congregate in the old ballroom where, rice, dhal and vegetables are served. Everyone is talking about one subject only; the fight for democracy. Helicopters have been flying around shooting at crowds of demonstrators. From the roof of the hotel smoke can be seen rising from many parts of the city. Every now and then gunshots can be heard. Tear gas has been used just outside Thamel on Tridevi Marg, and that when we were out during the one-hour lifting of the curfew.

Trekking groups and other tourists are holed up in hotels across the city. Some have fled the country already. One day foreign embassies arranged armed convoys of buses to take people to the airport for special emergency departures every couple of hours to Delhi and Bangkok. On the evening of the third night, a fire-burning protest is called. The aim, to burn every institution connected to the Panchayat system, which is now so unpopular that raw sentiment and frustration have boiled over on to the streets of the capital and across the country. At the hotel, people crowd around the television for news of events on the BBC World Service. Tension is visible on all the faces.

During the night there is more gunfire and shouting. At dawn, for no one has been sleeping, we hear the King has announced democracy for Nepal. There is joy and jubilation; the atmosphere has been transformed from one of impending doom to gaiety and celebration.

It's a wonderful day and the sunrise on a new era.

April 1990 Siân's story

At the same time that Bob was in Kathmandu, facing riots and curfews, I was up in the Khumbu. Having almost finished a Gokyo Lakes trek, my group had just returned to Namche Bazaar, where we met Per Lindstrom's group in a teashop. They were waiting to fly by balloon over Everest to Tibet, but the balloon was delayed by Customs problems. Never mind the fact that the country was in turmoil!

This was the first we had heard about any trouble in Kathmandu, for at this time communications were poor and our trekking staff had no radio. So it was a great shock to us all. We heard that people were being shot in the city, and the airport had been closed for a week. I didn't even know if Bob had reached Kathmandu. I had left him in London and he was going to fly out later, but he was due in on the day the airport was closed, so where was he?

In our group were two female army officers who had been trained in riot control. We had heard that Lukla airport had also been closed for a week, and our first thought was that there would probably be shortages in Lukla. What would be most uncomfortable for us, we wondered? The thought of no toilet paper was too dreadful to contemplate, and we guessed that with 70 or so people arriving in Lukla every day for a week and being unable to get out, toilet paper would probably be in short supply. So although it was obviously but a minor thing, we thought we had better make sure we had enough, and bought a roll in every little shop we passed on the way!

It was the last night party for our group. Nobody felt much like a party, with people being shot dead in Kathmandu, so we listened anxiously to the local radio.

13

And then we heard that King Birendra had declared that he would voluntarily relinquish power and allow democracy and a constitutional monarchy. This had happened in the middle of last night, and all Kathmandu was celebrating. It so happened that we were scheduled to fly out the next morning and, because of the way things worked, we would be flying out long before any of the people who had been waiting all week!

Finding it hard to believe our luck, we were actually on the second plane to fly out the following morning. There was a small cloud above the hill opposite Lukla and, without explanation, our pilot flew up towards Namche Bazaar, towards the dreamlike peak of Ama Dablam, in totally the opposite direction to what we were expecting. I thought, oh no, he's feeling suicidal, but what the hell, the view is fantastic. I might as well enjoy it. But would I see Bob again? Would he be in Kathmandu if we ever made it? Anyway, part of the worry was soon over as we circled over Namche, had a fabulous aerial view of the village, and headed southwest into the unknown.

And when we touched down on the tarmac, he was there, and nothing else mattered much...

In June 2001 King Birendra and almost his entire family were wiped out in a tragic shooting spree by his son, Crown Prince Dipendra. Many stories still abound about this terrible incident. His younger brother Gyanendra became king, and in turn his son became Crown Prince Paras some time later. In October 2002 King Gyanendra dissolved parliament and appointed his own government until elections could be held. Meanwhile the Maoist rebellion continued to threaten all parts of the country, and even in Kathmandu several bombs exploded not far from the tourist area of Thamel.

Coercion and intimidation were rife in the countryside and no solutions were in sight. In early 2003 a ceasefire was announced; in August the ceasefire was called off. The situation remained deadlocked in 2004, but most people were still full of hope.

We have come full circle. Is this the new age of Kali? What do the mysterious eyes know of the future?

We return to the legends of the lake and the voluminous lotus. What mysterious serpent has been aroused; what demons lurk in the heavens, waiting to unleash their anger on the once tranquil valley? We know from geological evidence that a lake did indeed exist in the valley, and that an earthquake probably enabled these waters to cut a path through the Chobar Gorge to the south of the valley near Dakshinkali.

The great stupa of Swayambhunath sits quietly, observing the daily scenes in all directions from its lofty perch. Monkeys guard its flanks and prayer flags adorn its brow. The sweet smell of incense pervades the air and the chanting of monks brings evocative, mystical sounds that carry us away in our imagination to a mysterious land of peace and tranquillity. The all-seeing, all-knowing eyes glance out from under a colourful shroud; the future too is shrouded in a haze that may envelop the land.

Garuda at Changu Narayan

15

Temple Guardian

CHAPTER THREE
Religion in the Kathmandu Valley

The religious life of the valley has been influenced tremendously by ideas from both India and Tibet, as a result of the trade and mixing of cultures.

Nepal was not prey to the destructive Muslim invasions of India, except in 1349, being virtually cut off from the Indian subcontinent by vast tracts of impenetrable forests. Malaria on its southern borders, and the Siwalik Hills and Mahabharat ranges all added to the difficulties. To the north, the massive barrier of the Himalayas also stood to defy the encroachment of outside civilisations. But there have always been passes and trade routes across the Himalayas and, indeed, access across the Terai in the south. Traders and men of religion have always continued to brave such obstacles in order to trade and spread their ideas. So, despite all these natural barriers, Nepalese culture was still subjected to a wealth of ideas, both from inside and outside.

Over the centuries, India was ruled by many Hindu dynasties and invaded by Muslims. Buddhism lost sway both to Islam and to the entrenched Hindu culture and religion in India. However, along with Jainism, the Buddhist ideas did survive these Hindu and Muslim onslaughts and continued to influence many parts of India, as well as the valleys of Nepal to the north. The Jains have much in common with Buddhists, believing in particular that all life forms are sacred and should not be killed.

Much later the Moghals, another Muslim dynasty that emanated from Ghazni in modern-day Afghanistan, held power in India. Buddhism continued to develop, and different schools of thought evolved. Two branches spread out, across the Indian subcontinent as far west as Bamiyan in Afghanistan, and into Southeast Asia as well as north into China and across to Japan. In India, Buddhism always competed with Hinduism, and did not come to rival that great religion. In Nepal Buddhism was stronger, although much modified in expression.

17

Hinduism has changed very little over the centuries, despite many other ideas that have arisen there. Perhaps surprisingly, one of the basic tenets of Hinduism is that there is only one true God; the same God who is also worshipped by Muslims, Christians and Jews alike. In popular Hinduism, the three main aspects of God are depicted by the Trimurti (the one with three forms) - Brahma, the Creator; Vishnu, the Preserver; and Shiva, the Destroyer. Within these three aspects, God's representation is further subdivided into hundreds of gods and goddesses and their various vehicles and dwelling places. So in all the festivals where we see worshipping of one or other of the gods and goddesses, people are actually worshipping the one God in various different forms.

In Kathmandu, Pashupatinath is the main Hindu temple; Boudhanath is the main Buddhist temple, while Swayambhunath is worshipped by both Hindus and Buddhists alike. As well as the Hindu and Buddhist temples, there is also a mosque, Sikh temple and a Christian church, and all religions coexist in perfect harmony.

Hinduism in Nepal

Much of the Hindu religious ideals have come from the ancient Indian Sanskrit texts, the four Vedas. In essence the ideas of Hinduism are based upon the idea that everything in the universe is connected, and that one action anywhere will cause another to occur, maybe elsewhere. This is, in terms of people, called Karma. It means that one should be continually aware of one's deeds in life being the instrument of further reaction. In the endless cycle of rebirth, one should strive to be a better person in this life. Bad Karma leads to a lower class/caste for the next life. The Hindu gods are all one, but each is venerated for a different aspect of the life cycle and one's own actions.

The worship of the Hindu gods is central to most of the population of Nepal and also in the Kathmandu Valley, where the Newari people adhere to both Hindu and Buddhist beliefs. The nature of Hinduism in the Kathmandu Valley has been much modified and integrated with Buddhist ideas. Within the valley are those who adhere to a pure form of Hindu belief, others are Buddhist, and between the two are the vast majority of the population. The worship of Bhairab is particularly strong in Nepal.

To understand the worship of Hindu gods in Nepal, we first need to understand what the gods represent and what their function is in society.

The Gods and Goddesses

There are three main gods, the trinity of Hindu worship and beliefs. Lord Shiva, the god of destruction, is one of the most important aspects of the Hindu trinity, the other two being Brahma (god of creation) and Vishnu (god of preservation.) These three gods can manifest in many forms, both male and female. Pashupati, the Lord of Beasts, is one of Shiva's many forms. Vishnu is also worshipped in Nepal. A form of Vishnu can be seen at Budhanilkantha, to north of the city, where a sleeping version is resplendent with snakes (the nagas) interwoven with the god. The Shah Kings of Nepal, like the earlier Malla Kings, are considered to be reincarnates of Vishnu and are not permitted to view this image. (It is rumoured that Crown Prince Dipendra did visit the sleeping Vishnu, and many people believe that this brought on the tragedy of June 2001.) The third life form or god is Brahma, but he is not active, having been the great creator in the beginning.

The God Brahma: There are some people who worship Brahma, but they are very much in the minority. Brahma created the universe but has no more work to be done. Brahma has four faces, but only three are visible. The four faces represent the four Vedas. His fifth head has been chopped off, according to one legend. He carries among his things the Veda book, a water vessel and the beads of time. Brahma's consort is **Saraswati**, the goddess of learning, knowledge and poetry. She is benign and also appears as **Brahmi** and **Brahmayani**. Brahmayani is pride and rides a goose. She carries a watering can and beads.

The God Shiva: In the Hindu pantheon of gods and goddesses, we have **Shiva** and **Shakti**. Strictly speaking Shakti is not a goddess, but the female aspect of union. Both have a destructive capability that is the primary subject of worship for the Hindu people of Nepal. Shiva and Shakti have many forms. Each form illustrates a different temperament and nature of the deities. Shiva is the god of destruction but, combined with Shakti, he is the one who has the power to recreate.

Bhairab is Shiva in his most gruesome, monstrous form, a god bent on death and destruction. He is terror. Bhairab is black, sometimes blue and angry. In his white form he is so terrible that he must be hidden from view,

Shiva-Parvati Temple, Kathmandu Durbar Square

Bhairab

daring only to be viewed once a year during the Indra Jatra festivities. The legend of Bhairab is linked to the story of creation. In this version Shiva

20

decapitated his father Brahma's fifth head in fury, for lusting after his own daughter. Shiva roamed the universe. He could have performed no greater sin. Shiva moved aimlessly, destitute and carrying Brahma's skull as his begging bowl. When he came to Varanasi he atoned for his mistake by bathing in holy pools. Punished sufficiently for his sins, he had to leap ahead of time to become Mahakala, and then to transcend time he became Bhairab. Bhairab represents the demonic forces of evil and one must strive to placate him.

Pashupati is Shiva as lord of the beasts. **Mahadev** is Shiva; he is the supreme lord, the serene aspect. When Shiva is in a playful mode he is tempting, through dance, sometimes erotic. In this form he is **Nataraj** with fourteen arms. Nataraj, the dancing Shiva, represents the rhythm of the cosmos as sun, moon, earth, wind etc.

Shakti is the female energy of Shiva, giving him life. The following goddesses are all different manifestations of Shiva's female consort. **Parvati** is Shiva's benign wife. Together they view the world of the Durbar Square in Kathmandu. **Kali** is the destructive dark blue goddess, with a necklace of skulls. She is angry and revengeful, seeking the obliteration of all in her path. **Durga**, who cuts a swathe in wrathful anger, is another form of Kali whose face remains outwardly calm. Dashain is the festival that celebrates this deathly anger with blood sacrifices. Bloodthirsty **Taleju** vanished and now resides as an incarnate in the virgin Kumari child goddess. The peacock is the Kumari's vehicle. Another version of Shiva's consort is **Bhairavi** the warrior goddess; as **Sundari** she is beauty. She is **Bhagawati** and **Bhadrakali**. As **Mohini** she is an erotic vision, a temptress who dances naked to arouse passion. There are many forms of Shakti; some Tantrics worship ten forms of Shakti in meditation. **Uma Maheshwara** is Shiva and Shakti together. **Mahadevi** is a goddess liked to Shakti and Tantra.

Kali is the black one, the force that stops time. She is the aspect of destruction, divine wisdom that seeks an end to illusion. She has a hunger for life. She even subjugates Shiva by dancing on him. She devours all in her path.

The Story of Durga

Mahisa, lord of the demons, defeated the gods. But their energy rose up like a burning mountain, and all their energy focused as the goddess Durga. She killed the demon, despite his assuming different forms; lion, buffalo and human.

The lion is the vehicle of Durga, and buffaloes are killed at the festival of Dashain; fortunately, human sacrifice is no longer carried out!

Ganesh is the son of Shiva and Parvati. But why does he have the head of an elephant? Legends recount that Parvati gave birth to Ganesh while Shiva was away from home for a long time. When he returned, he saw the child and assumed that Parvati had had an affair with another man. In a furious rage, he chopped off Ganesh's head and threw it far, far away. Distraught, Parvati explained that he was in fact Shiva's son. Shiva was now also distraught and vowed to give Ganesh the head of the first living being that passed their home. This just happened to be an elephant. Ganesh is worshipped to give happiness and a good life.

Shrew/rat at Jal Vinayak

Kumar is Ganesh's younger brother. He is also known as Karttikeya in Nepal and Skanda in India, and is the god of war. See festivals for the months of May/June for the story of his birth.

Nandi the bull is the vehicle of Shiva. Nandi means 'giving delight' and embodies inner strength. The **Rat** is the vehicle of Ganesh. The rat is sometimes said to be a shrew or mouse.

The God Vishnu

Vishnu is the preserver of life. Vishnu has ten incarnations (avatars). He is most often found in the valley as **Narayan**. The visions of Vishnu in Nepal are as follows: -

Machha Narayan, or **Matsya**, the fish, is the first avatar.

Kurma the tortoise man, the second avatar, is rarely seen.

Varaha is the boar-headed third avatar. His consort is **Varahi**.

Narasingha, the half-man/half-lion image, is the fourth avatar.

Vamana is the fifth avatar; he is the dwarf version of Vishnu. The dwarf represents ignorance.

Parashurama is Vishnu in human form, the sixth avatar.

Rama is the seventh and is famous from the Indian epic, Ramayana. His wife is **Sita**. **Krishna**, the eighth avatar, is the amorous vision of Vishnu who plays a flute. He is often blue in colour and is famous for chasing around after girls of the field, the cow herders or gopis. Surprisingly though, he is not seen in erotic poses. **Radha** is one of Krishna's wives and **Rukmini** another. **Jagannath** is Krishna as Lord of the Universe.

Buddha is the ninth avatar of Vishnu. Buddha came to purify the moral decline of the world. **Harihari-vahan Lokeshvara** is Vishnu in the Buddhist context.

Kalki is the last and tenth avatar of Vishnu, who is yet to come.

As a complete aside here, it has been noted that these ancient avatars of Vishnu correspond to the same order that thousands of years later Charles Darwin set out in his theory of biological evolution.

Visvarupa is the all-encompassing Vishnu.

Vishnu's consort is **Lakshmi**, goddess of wealth, and thus very popular in Nepal. She has four arms and is worshipped on the new moon of November during the Tihar festivities. **Vasundhara** is linked to Lakshmi, and sometimes is seen as a three-headed goddess. **Annapurna** is another goddess of the earth, food and plenty.

Garuda is the vehicle of Vishnu. He is a man-bird figure and is found in many places in Nepal. Normally he appears mainly human with wings behind, but sometimes he has the head of a bird. **Vainateya** is Garuda in human form.

Balarama is Krishna's older brother. Hari Krishna is a movement connected with Krishna.

Embrace of the Gods

The Shakti-Shiva embrace is the coupling of the lingam and the yoni. Shiva is the cosmic male. His sex organ is the lingam represented by a pillar, column or obelisk. Shakti is the cosmic female; her organ is represented by a circle or dish. The Shiva lingam is the cosmic mountain, the mountains of the Himalayas. The Ganges river represents the flow of energy from heaven to earth. It descends from the head of Shiva, at Mt Kailash. In other cultures, the yab-yum of Tibet and the yin-yang are similar embraces. Everything comes from the union of generative forces, the sacred couple as creation itself.

All the erotic art forms of the Kathmandu Valley revolve around the central theme of union, the embrace of the male and female. This can be depicted in a multitude of ways; whether it be a couple alone, or with extra figures or even animals, all illustrate the act of embrace. The Shiva-Shakti embrace is the embrace of creation. Eroticism ignites the passion of desire and union for creativity. Physical activity can also bring vitality, sensuality and a renewed sense of well-being. Connected in the Shiva-Shakti embrace, energy flows in a circle to enrich the body and fulfil its needs. It brings sex and consciousness together. Ultimately it is said to lead to enlightenment of the divine mind, transforming the physical experience into spiritual awareness.

Taleju Temple, Kathmandu

Other (mainly) Hindu Gods, Goddesses and Deities of the Valley

The gods and goddesses of the Kathmandu Valley are intriguing. There are far too many to list, but we need to explain some of the more common deities that adorn the myriad of shrines in the valley.

Taleju is a goddess, a consort of Shiva, as we have mentioned. She had special significance to the Malla Kings, who built so many Taleju and Degutaleju temples. The origins of Taleju are in the Ramayana, as a Yantra geometric representation. The Yantra was worshipped by Indra but stolen by Ravena. It was retrieved by Rama and taken to Ayodhya. A goddess told Rama to throw it into the river. Later it reappeared at Simra in the Terai of Nepal. After the brief Muslim attack it came to Bhaktapur, still as Taleju. The Mallas adopted Taleju as their deity. Taleju is a Tantric goddess. She has no known form of her own, but is seen as Durga or Bhagawati.

Indra is the god of heaven, the natural elements and of rain, and he is worshipped for good harvests. He is linked to Shiva and rides an elephant. His weapons are thunder and lightning. He expels the demons of drought. His consort is **Indrayani**, whose sisters are **Kankeshwari**, **Neta Ajima** and **Bhadrakali**. Indrayani is sometimes called **Luti Ajima**, a grandmother goddess who curbs dysentery. She must be very busy out here!

Yama is the god of death. He sits in judgement and appears in three forms. Yama is also **Kala**. He accompanies beings to the other world as king of the invisible world, and is thus the god of judgment. **Yami**, his consort, also came as the first human, as the first mortal. Both come from **Surya**, the sun god. Worship of Surya, one of the early Vedic gods, has been mostly superseded by worship of Vishnu.

Hanuman is the monkey god and is very popular in the Kathmandu Valley. Hanuman helped Rama to rescue Sita and destroy the demon Ravena. In Nepal he is covered in red vermilion, has a red cloth and often has a red or gold umbrella over his head. He is often represented by a rather shapeless stone or rock.

Chhepu is a dragon-like figure holding his food of snakes/nagas in his mouth or talons. He is found on many toranas above temple doors. He is one of Garuda's two brothers. He has a head but no body. Why should this be so? Various legends tell his story. One says it is because his mother saw him prematurely, before his body had been completely formed. Her husband had told her to wait, and not look upon her son until an auspicious time would make him brave, truthful and superior.

Another legend recalls a time when Chhepu disappeared from the earth. He feared to see the time when evil triumphed over good; when Vishnu, appearing as his tenth avatar Kalki, the destroyer, would annihilate the world. Manjushri asked to see Chhepu, and when Chhepu came along, Manjushri began to draw him in secret. But Chhepu realised what was happening, and disappeared before Manjushri could draw his body. So Chhepu has no body form.

Kirtimukha is another guardian figure, similar to, and easily confused with, Chhepu. He is frequently found on the toranas of Buddhist shrines.

Mahadevi means the great goddess (maha means great and devi means goddess). She is worshipped in two aspects, benign and creative, or violent and destructive. Female strength is in procreation, and is the source of life that in itself carries its own inevitable destruction.

The **Astha Matrikas** are the eight (astha), ten or even twelve mother goddesses. They are connected to the forces of evil and ignorance, good and knowledge. They are Tantric in nature. The Matrikas are the Shaktis who give power to gods, including Shiva. Each represents a vice such as violence or disease. Their existence now is probably associated with worship before Hinduism. The mother goddesses were the driving forces of creation. Later Tantra used them to emphasise the role of the Shakti female principle. The Astha Matrika goddesses' temples were originally found around the settlements of the valley as the protecting deities.

Some of the Matrikas are as follows: —

Kaumari, consort of Kumar (not to be confused with the Kumari), represents bad temper. She appears with three eyes and two to twelve legs.

Vaishnavi is envy, she rides Garuda.

Maheshvari is greed.

Varahi, consort of Varaha, relates to lust and is depicted with the head of a boar. She has four hands and is derived from Vishnu.

Chamunda relates to blindness and is linked to Kali and to Yama. She is the sixth deity, rides on a corpse and is red. She was created by Durga and killed the demons, Chanda and Munda.

Sweta Kali, also called **Nara Devi**, is a mother goddess.

Two others are called **Mahaipi** and **Chwasa Ajima**.

Indrayani, consort of Indra, represents rage and holds a bolt of lightning. She is both grandmother and mother goddess in different contexts.

Maitidevi is classed by some as a mother goddess.

Sometimes **Bhadrakali** is a mother goddess, and sometimes a consort of Shiva. **Kankeshwari** is another.

The Astha Matrikas require constant propitiation, through periodic pujas with offerings of auspicious foodstuffs, to secure their active protection from attack by spirits, deities or witches. These often-fierce female deities, who must counter fierce supernatural forces, can thus be considered mediators between the realms of the deity and that of the lower demonic force.

Mahalakshmi is another of the mother goddesses. She is not menacing, despite her sixteen arms. She is linked to the goddess Durga, and is often depicted standing on a lion. Mahalakshmi is the embodiment of the three aspects of the creation of life. These are spirituality, purity and that which is hidden in the dark out of sight, the void. Any of the goddesses will have some of her attributes. In some forms she has a miniature lingam on her head with three eyes and four arms.

Ajima goddesses are the different grandmother goddesses.

Mahakala is the great blackness identified with Bhairab. In Buddhism, Mahakala is one of the eight aspects of terror and can be exceedingly ugly and ferocious in art forms. **Mahakali** is the great blackness, an extreme form of Kali.

Kubera is the lord of wealth and guardian of the treasures of the world. Buddhists in Nepal worship Kubera as **Jambhala**. He sits on a dragon sideways, and is attended by a mongoose that vomits jewels.

Kama is the god of love and desire. Kama was born from the heart of Brahma, to seduce Shiva and make him succumb to Parvati. He is also called **Yaksha** and a son of Vishnu in later stories.

Ganga is the goddess of the rivers, who is a sister of Parvati but could not become Shiva's consort.

The following gods are the older **Vedic gods** who predate the more recent Hindu Trinity and associated goddesses: -

Agni is the god of fire. Agni is used for some fire rituals and can acquire human form.

Surya is the sun god, who lives in the east and brightens up the mornings. He is represented in art as a disc with rays, smiling.

Soma is a god of the moon and the son of **Varuna**, god of the oceans. Soma is also known as **Chandra**, who rises up from the oceans.

Vayu is the god of winds. His attribute is the banner.

Nagas are symbols of power, for as serpents they can kill. They can also lose layers of skin and regenerate, like immortal gods who carry sacrifices to heaven. The Nagas are the rain givers, the guardians of water, and are found everywhere in the valley. They are the snakes and serpents that adorn many idols and temples. The nagas are probably connected with the earliest animistic forms of worship in the valley.

Yoni/Lingam

Buddhism in Nepal

Although Buddhism is considered as a religion, it is in many ways more a way of living, a code of practice, a search for peace of mind and an end to suffering.

Buddhism is believed to have been the first religion of Nepal and was later modified by influences from India and Tibet. Although Buddhism appears quite different from Hinduism at first sight, Buddha is considered by Hindus to be an Avatar—an incarnation of God. In one of the famous Hindu lyric poems, Vishnu is praised as the great God who, in the guise of Buddha, taught us kindness to all living beings and prohibited animal sacrifices. There are indeed some important doctrinal differences between Hinduism and Buddhism, but Buddha himself lived and died a Hindu and the two religions are closely intertwined.

Prince Gautama Siddhartha, who became the Buddha, was born the son of a king near present day Lumbini in southern Nepal. His early life was one of luxury; he married the daughter of a neighbouring Raja. In his twenty-ninth year he was suddenly aware that there was more to life than he knew, so he left his wife and newborn son to take up the life of an ascetic. He wandered far and wide listening to sages, wise men and Brahmin priests, but could find no solace. After many temptations and much thoughtful meditation he became enlightened, choosing a pathway of acceptance of all suffering. Thus began Buddhism, in approximately 600 BC.

Tantra and the form of Buddhism known as Vajrayana later influenced some of the original Buddhist practices. Many adherents in India decried the general liberalisation of pure Buddhism by Tantric ideas. Some believe the Tantric ideas predate both Buddhism and Hinduism, being both ritualistic and pagan in their ancient format. However, these corrupted practices came northwards from India, as well as the Hindu ideas. Newari Buddhism, probably the oldest religion of the valley, has some ideas associated with Hindu castes. Tibetan Buddhist Tantra developed around the eleventh century, with the Kalachakra elements that relate to the Kangyur Tibetan scripts. Kalachakra is the protector who turns the wheel of life.

Tibetan Buddhism incorporated a lot of the demonic worship of the original occult Bonpo animistic ideas that formed the earliest religious practices in Tibet. Over the centuries, this modified form of Buddhism returned southwards from Tibet to further influence the religious practices in Nepal and, in particular, the Kathmandu Valley. Tantric influences are strong in the valley and have also made their contribution to religious developments in Nepal. It was these Tantric themes that had ultimately the most influence over the religious institutions in the valley.

In the early mornings, as the first rays of the sun strike the great Buddhist stupas of Swayambhunath and Boudhanath, one can almost feel this veneer of Tantric mist, a cloak of ritual, of esoteric vibrations.

Buddhist Idols, Deities and Other Terminology

Adi Buddha is the Buddha without beginning or end, the infinite self-created Buddha who is present at Swayambhunath. The eyes of the stupa represent the Adi Buddha; the primordial Buddha. Vajradhara is the name of the Adi Buddha when he is represented either in single form or in yab-yum with his Shakti. Occasionally the Adi Buddha can be seen nude; in this form he is called Samantabhadra and is also recognised as such by the Tibetan Nyingma-pa sect.

Shakyamuni is the pure image of the mortal Buddha, Gautama Siddhartha, born in Nepal.

The **Dhyani Buddhas** face the four cardinal directions, meditating, and are abstract images encompassing the universe. These five mystical Buddhas are found in the Mahayana form of Buddhism that developed over the subcontinent. The Dhyani Buddhas were created from the meditation and wisdom of the Adi Buddha. The Dhyani Buddhas in turn evolved into the Dhyani Bodhisattvas who gave creation to the universe. Some of these then gave us the human or mortal teachers.

Vairochana is the first Dhyani Buddha and resides in the stupa sanctum. He is the cosmic element, who cannot be shown. On occasion he appears on the east side of large stupas (e.g. Swayambhu).

Akshobhya is the Dhyani Buddha who sits facing east. He is regarded as the second Dhyani Buddha in Nepal. He looks similar to Ratna Sambhava, but his right hand has its palm facing inwards.

Amitabha is the oldest of the Dhyani Buddhas, he always faces west on a stupa. The Amitabha Buddha is linked to Shakyamuni, the earthly Buddha.

Aparmita is a version of Amitabha with his hands clasping a vase on his lap. The Panchen Lama is considered to be his earthly representative.

Amoghasiddhi is the Dhyani Buddha who always faces north on a stupa or chaitya. Usually a serpent with seven heads stands behind him. This Dhyani Buddha is linked to the future Buddha, Maitreya.

Ratna Sambhava is the Dhyani Buddha who faces south; his right hand has its palm facing outwards. He is yellow in colour.

Vajrasattva is the sixth Dhyani Buddha. He is the priest for the other five, and is only found separately from his disciples. He carries a vajra and a bell. Vajrasattva is considered to be the Adi Buddha by the Kadam-pa Tibetan sect.

Amitayus is the Buddha of Boundless Life; an aspect of Amitabha; the Buddha associated with longevity practice and empowerment of longevity. He is found seated with a vase in his hands.

Maitreya Buddha is the future Buddha to come and appears in a number of monasteries. His colour is yellow or gold and he is said to be preparing to come to earth.

A **Bodhisattva** is a saint or disciple of Buddha who has delayed the attainment of Nirvana and has remained to teach. They are found in the Mahayana path of Buddhism. The term can be confusing. Translated literally, it comes from Bodhi, meaning highest consciousness, and sattva, meaning reality or essence within the living.

Lokeshvara is a lord of the world and has 108 different versions (bodhisattvas). Avalokiteshvara is the most commonly found version, being the one who came back to earth to save mankind. Lokeshvara appears in some forms with two or many heads.

Avalokiteshvara is a popular and famous bodhisattva. He is called **Chenresig** in Tibet. He has renounced Nirvana, the end of the cycle of rebirth. He embodies compassion (Karuna) and remains on earth to counter distress and suffering. He is believed by many to be the creator of our universe. Avalokiteshvara in one aspect is quite commonly seen in visual form with eleven heads and eyes on his hands. The **Dalai Lama** is considered to be his earthly representative.

Padmapani is another version of Lokeshvara linked to the Dhyani Buddha, Amitabha. He is seen with the lotus displayed prominently. He is generally white, but also can be red in one version.

Machhendranath is the powerful deity of the rainmakers; he is worshipped by both Buddhists and Hindus for a good harvest and for a season without droughts. He is the god of mercy and is hailed as Karunamaya, the compassionate one. Machhendranath can appear in two forms, white as **Seto Machhendranath** and red as **Rato Machhendranath**. In his white form, in Buddhism he is Avalokiteshvara. He is also worshipped by Hindu devotees of both Vishnu and Shiva. His red form is only recognised by Buddhists; he is Bung Deo or Padmapani.

Popular legend has it that his disciple, Gorakhnath, had created a drought in the valley by sitting on and imprisoning the nine nagas, the rain-givers. Machhendranath was then brought to the valley as a black bee in an urn, protected by four powerful Bhairabs. When Gorakhnath heard that his guru was coming, he stood up and came to pay homage to Machhendranath; so the snake nagas were freed and the rains came. *Bu* means birthplace in Newari, so the village of Bungamati was named as Lord Machhendranath's birthplace.

This is all supposed to have taken place in the reign of King Narendradeva (644-680). Different versions of the legend exist in India. In Tibet he is called Jowo Dzamling Karmo, the white Lord of the World. A legend in Tibet relates Machhendranath to Srongtsen Gampo, whose two wives became the white and green Taras.

The Seto Machhendranath sometimes embraces the green Tara. In the Buddhist union they embrace in the yab-yum position, with Tara usually depicted as a small nymph. Seeking to bring his powers alive; seeking to overcome suffering. The yab-yum is rarely seen in idol form in the Kathmandu Valley. Usually the embracing figures appear only in paintings, tangkas and devotional artefacts, and now even on computer mouse mats!

Tara is sacred to Hindus and Buddhists alike in Nepal. She represents the maternal aspect, symbolising fertility, purity and compassion. Tara can appear in different colours, red, green, white, gold, and as Kali, dark blue.

Each represents a different aspect of her nature. There are considered to be twenty-one aspects or forms of Tara.

The **White Tara** was born of a tear from the bodhisattva, Avalokiteshvara, a compassionate saviour and disciple of Buddha past. She is a consort of Vairochana, the first Dhyani Buddha. She is worshipped for long life, and for healing.

The **Green Tara** is most often associated with the Nepalese **Princess Bhrikuti** who married a Tibetan King. She is worshipped for liberation from danger. She is also linked spiritually to Amoghasiddhi, the Dhyani Buddha, and inspires good in women.

Tara also has a ferocious form called **Ekajata**. She is seen standing on a corpse, has a third eye, is dwarf-like, ugly and is usually blue. Ugratara also means a terrible version of Tara and is linked to the Vajra Yogini of Sankhu. The rare **Red Tara** is called Kurukulla.

Vajratara and **Prajnaparmita** (confers wisdom) emanate from the five Dhyani Buddhas.
Prajnaparmita is probably the most popular deity within Vajrayana. She is the goddess of superior wisdom and can shine a light on the way to Nirvana.

Vajrapani is a spiritual son of Dhyani Buddha Akshobhya, and is a god of rain (*pani*). He is protector of the nagas and is linked to Garuda in legend and in aspect. He carries a vajra.

Vasundhara is the consort of Jambhala and linked to the Hindu goddess of wealth Lakshmi. She holds the vase, mudra, jewels and a sheaf of rice straw. She is a popular deity in Nepal.

Dipanker is an unusual deity. He is the enlightener, and is normally red in colour. At his birth, bright lights appeared miraculously. He is said to be a Buddha of a previous cosmic or life cycle.

Manjushri is the god of divine wisdom. According to legend, with his massive sword he slashed open the Chobar Gorge to drain the lake that once was the Kathmandu Valley. According to tradition he is a Chinese saint. To worship Manjushri gives intellect and intelligence. Manjushri is a popular bodhisattva and is considered to be the first divine teacher of Buddhism, giving inspiration.

Mahakala carries a trident and is an emanation of Dhyani Buddhas in the terrible Tantric form. He is seen rather like the terrible Hindu god Bhairab and often tramples on bodies or corpses.

Vajra Yogini is a female goddess linked to Bhairab and to Tantric Buddhism. She can appear in different forms. Sometimes she is serene, bewitching and nude. Sometimes she is seen carrying her own head in her left hand, a head she herself has cut off. There are said to be four such idols in the valley; all are Tantric and potentially fearsome. The images at Sankhu and Pharping, as well as an unseen one at Gujeshwari, are three of the Vajra Yoginis. A fourth is at Vidyeshvari. They often actually appear as beautiful images but have a hidden wrath.

Vidhyadhari is a spirit or demigod with Tantric magic powers and is skilled in yoga. She appears like a dancing nymph standing on a corpse. She has two arms. One of her two legs is bent backwards. She is related to the Vajra Yoginis. Is her hidden shrine the fourth of the Vajra Yogini shrines of the valleys that is not evident?

Vajradhara is one of the highest deities. He appears as single or in the rare Buddhist YabYum male-female embrace. Vajradhara is considered by the Tibetan Geluk-pa sect to be the primordial or Adi Buddha.

Vajra Varahi is a red goddess who embodies the five wisdoms and pleasures. She appears nude and is sometimes seen trampling on Bhairab. She was a consort of Padma Sambhava / Guru Rinpoche.

Nagarjun was a great Buddhist philosopher and mastered the sciences and also magic art. The Sakya-pa sect can be traced to him. He is usually known as the founder of Mahayana Buddhism.

Padma Sambhava / Guru Rinpoche The lotus-born Tantric master who established Vajrayana Buddhism in Tibet in the 8th - 9th century at the invitation of King Trisong Deutsen. The Nyingma-pa Red Hat sect began at around the same time. In Tibet he tamed hostile spirits and made it possible to build Samye monastery. Although he was able to learn the teachings spontaneously, he pretended to have to study in order to instil confidence in ordinary people. And he hid various important teachings in Tibet, Nepal and Bhutan, in order that they may be revealed for future generations in years to come. He was also known as **Padma Kara**.

Vajrayana Buddhism is a later development of Buddhism. It postulates that every being is a Buddha and can strive for his own enlightenment. The path is the Vajrayana. In the Kathmandu Valley, much of the Vajrayana path includes elements of Tantra.

Vajra is the thunderbolt, a path through the mists, as it were, to clear a way for wisdom. It destroys ignorance. The Vajra symbol is a metal object and is found at many temples and shrines. It is the symbol of Indra, and in Tantra it is the male principle.

Vajra Seat, Bodhgaya. This is the diamond seat under the bodhi tree at Bodhgaya, where Buddha Shakyamuni attained enlightenment.

Dakini is a class of demon goddesses who can fly. She is the female partner in Tantric union, a female Tantric deity who protects and serves the Buddhist doctrine and practitioners; a spiritual being. The Vajra Varahi and Vajra Yogini deities are often classified as Dakinis.

Daka is the male counterpart of dakini; a male practitioner of Vajrayana.

The Early Life of Padma Sambhava

In Sanskrit, *Padma* means *lotus flower*, and *Sambhava* means *born from*.

Why was Padma Sambhava so important? With his great spiritual power, he created the conditions for the propagation of the teachings of Vajrayana Buddhism in this world. And he hid various important teachings in order that they may be revealed for future generations — even to this present day.

In the Sutra of Predictions in Magadha, the Buddha said:-
I will pass away to eradicate the view of permanence.
But twelve years from now, to clear away the view of nihilism,
I shall appear from a lotus in the immaculate Lake Kosha
As a noble son to delight the king
And turn the Dharma wheel of the unexcelled essential meaning.

The following is the story of the miraculous birth of Padma Sambhava: -

Once upon a time there was a king, Indrabodhi, who had no son. He was a good and generous man, always trying to feed all the poor people in his land, but one day his treasury was empty and he could do no more. He knew that on an island lived the naga king's daughter, who possessed a great jewel that would satisfy all wishes. It was said that anyone who practised generosity for the right reasons might receive the jewel. So the king went off to seek it.

Crossing oceans and fending off demons, he finally reached the golden island and, through meditation and good thoughts, was able to retrieve the precious jewel. On his way back home, he saw an eight-year-old boy sitting alone on another island, carrying a vajra in one hand and a lotus in the other.

The king spoke to him, and realised from his answers that he must be a miraculous emanation, so he took him for his son. When he returned home he asked the jewel to restock his treasury, which was miraculously done. Then the king gave alms to all who asked; clothes for the cold, food for the hungry, and a shower of gems for the poor. He told them all they must study and practise Mahayana Buddhism.

But as the prince grew up, he realised he could not benefit the people by ruling the kingdom. So he killed the son of

one of the ministers, in order that he would be banished from the kingdom. He was sent to live in the charnel grounds among the corpses. Local customs meant that the corpses were brought wrapped in cloth, and the prince used this cloth as clothing to wrap around his body.

One day he heard that nearby there was an evil king named Shakraraja, who was forcing his people on to a path to hell. So the prince went there and wore the skin of the corpses as his clothing; he ate the flesh of the males and copulated with the females. He brought everyone under his power and was known as the Rakshasa demon. The evil king tried to kill him, but he escaped. He went on to various other charnel grounds, being empowered and blessed by the dakinis. All the spirits promised to be his servants and he became a powerful yogi.

He reflected on the needs of future generations. Then he approached two monks, who were afraid when they saw him. But he said, "I am not doing any more evil, please accept me," and he handed over his weapons. They sent him to their master, who named him Shakya Senge and taught him more Yoga Tantra.

After this he was sent to meet the nun Kungamo. Even her maidservant had amazing powers, cutting open her torso to reveal the 42 peaceful deities in her upper body and 58 wrathful ones in her lower torso. When he finally reached the nun, she swallowed him as the syllable HUNG and then emitted him through the secret lotus, empowered externally as Amitabha and internally as Avalokiteshvara. She named him Loden Chogsey.

Loden Chogsey realised that he would need a consort in order to practise the Secret Mantra, so he went to the land of Sahor and found a beautiful young maiden. They went together to the Cave of Maratika, and after three months they had a vision of Amitayus. He blessed them both, master Padma as the daka Hayagriva and his

consort as Vajra Varahi. They then went back to Sahor, where the people recognised him and tried to kill them both by fire. But the fire was still burning after nine days — when the people came closer to look, the fire blazed up and burned the entire royal palace. In the midst of the flames sat Padma and his consort, unscathed. So they were released and worshipped, and everyone practised the Buddha dharma.

Now he returned to his homeland and the same thing happened; the people recognised him as the man who had killed the son of their minister, and tried to burn them both. This time the fire was still burning after twenty-one days. All were afraid to go and look, but the king, who was Padma Sambhava's father, thought, "If he really is a miraculous emanation, then he should not burn." So he went to have a look. Sitting in the middle of a huge lake was Padma and his consort, adorned with garlands of skulls in order to liberate beings through compassion. The king was filled with wonder.

Later, in about 747 AD, Padma was invited to Tibet by King Trisong Detsen, in order to subjugate the local spirits and yakshas. These Bonpo spirits constantly attempted to destroy his attempts to build the holy temple of Samye monastery. But on his journey he manifested as a fierce character, terrifying all who saw him. In this way Samye monastery was finally built.

He is generally credited as being the founder of Tibetan Lamaism, mixing Mahayana Buddhism and the existing Bonpo cults together. Padma was a teacher of the Tantric school. In Tibet he is revered by the Red Hat or old school, Nyingma-pa sect, and is known as Guru Rinpoche.

After creating Samye monastery, he intended to return to India, but in fact he did not do so for approximately 56 years, so it is said...

Tibetan Demon

Buddhist Sects

Nyingma-pa is the oldest Tibetan Buddhist sect; its adherents are known as the Red Hat sect. Guru Rinpoche is generally considered to be the founder of Lamaism in Tibet. At Boudhanath we find a few monasteries following this sect.

Sakya-pa is another Tibetan sect, which is found in the Kathmandu Valley, notably at Boudhanath within the main circular precincts.

Kadam-pa is another smaller sect that was developed by Atisha and his disciple Drontonpa about a thousand years ago. Atisha was an Indian prince, a priest and an intellectual. He journeyed to Tibet and later became a great teacher and Tibetan icon.

Kagyu-pa is a sect founded by the mystic Marpa, a disciple of Atisha. Milarepa became the Kagyu-pa's great saint, as well as being a hermit and poet. In his early life he practised black magic. After he reformed he lived in isolation in the Himalayas. His cave is thought to be near Nyalam, just across the border from Nepal, in Tibet.

Gelug-pa is the Yellow Hat sect of the Dalai Lama. Earlier reforms by Atisha were refined by Tsong Khapa in the 14th century. Tsong Khapa is held to be the initiator and reformer of this sect. This form of Buddhism reverted to a more purist format, bringing a higher degree of morality and discipline to the monk body. The first monastery was established at Ganden near Lhasa.

Other Definitions

A **Chaitya** is either a small box-like square temple with an image inside, or a small, stupa-style stone structure almost always with four Buddha figures on each side.

A **Chorten** is a similar structure, but is mostly found in the high Buddhist mountain country. Some chortens are seen at Swayambhunath.

A **Charnel ground** is a place where dead bodies are left to decompose or be eaten by wild animals. Frequented by ghosts and spirits, it is a place for advanced practitioners to progress in their realisation.

Dharmadhartu are usually hexagonal plinths with the lotus as decoration. They have almost flat tops, sometimes in stone or gilded. They represent many Buddhist deities and, put very simply, they are visual aids to worship. They are very common, particularly in Patan.

Samsara is the cycle of birth, death and rebirth. Ordinary reality, an endless cycle of frustration and suffering is the result of karma.

Dharma is the path to enlightenment; way of alleviating suffering.

Sangha is the support and guidance necessary on the way to enlightenment.

Tantra in Nepal

In Sanskrit, Tantra means liberation, an expansion of ideas. Taken literally, it means an expansion tool, a way of increasing the awareness of the mind to reach the divine level.

Some scholars believe that Tantric ideas can be traced to Stone Age art, which evolved from ritualistic pagan ideas. Its origins probably pre-date all the ancient religious concepts of India, as well as Hinduism and Buddhism. It was transmitted orally until around the 3rd century AD. Its earliest forms were integrated into witchcraft, shamanism, blood sacrifices and other pagan practices. Some of these pagan ideas have survived to manifest today in temple art, festivals and daily rituals.

Later, pagan Tantra was suffocated by new ideas. These new ideas, Hinduism and Buddhism, suggested that all life was a cycle of suffering and rebirth on a path to enlightenment. Tantric themes did influence Buddhism through the Vajrayana path and were still practised quite openly. Its liberal ideas suggested in effect, that 'paradise' was achievable 'now' and that each being could find his own path. Tantra in these forms was virtually obliterated in India by the Muslim invasions of the 12th and 13th centuries. The invaders found the idol worship and liberal concepts totally abhorrent. Hidden behind the Himalayas, though, Tantra survived in Tibet, Ladakh, Nepal and the remoter parts of Assam. See below.

Most forms of Tantra were subject to animistic ideas, with a corrupting of more idealistic thought. However, Tantra also developed in less pagan ways, having both physical and mental strands to reach a complete state of peace. Some people perform Tantric meditation, which does not involve any physical methods, but is purely visual and uses the imagination.

Everything in the physical world is seen as opposites of polarity. This is the Shiva-Shakti, male-female aspect. Duality is Tantra's prime direction. Within the male-female domain there is some overlap, but each is incomplete without the other. There is suffering. Tantra interweaves the two to make one. There are elements of the female within the male and vice-versa. Balance can only be achieved through the actions of both acting as one. In Tantra the coupling enables the fiery energies to join and the intellects to exchange in order to escape to a higher consciousness.

Tantra seeks to utilise the inner female power to save the world from destruction. One must strive to balance the male-female energy on earth to open up to the cosmos. Tantrics strongly worship the female, both as the true female and the feminine part of the male. Shiva is a corpse in Tantra, and only through union with the all-powerful female can the male attain consciousness to make him whole. Shakti gives him form by flowing through him. Do the erotic figures on the temples of Nepal awaken the power of Shakti to raise the powers of Shiva? The powers of destruction in Shiva are needed to lead to rebirth, re-growth and regeneration.

Some Hindu Tantrics worship ten different goddesses, believing that each represents an aspect of teaching and knowledge to aid self-realisation. Each of the ten paths or goddesses are forms of Shakti. There is a link here with the ancient worship of the goddess and mother goddess that some also believe predate the current religious concepts. In Nepal there are many manifestations of this theme in and on the temples of the Kathmandu valley.

In fact many temples and monasteries in Nepal are associated with Tantric forms and ideas. The great stupa of Swayambhunath, sacred to both Hindus and Buddhists, is veiled in a Tantric cloak. Its traditions, symbols and deities ooze with Tantric overtones.

Much of Tantra reaches to the esoteric, far beyond the confines of religion.

Tibetan Tantra

In Tibet, the Tantric ideas originally came from India, together with Buddhism, before the Muslim invasions south of the Himalayas. Tibetan Tantra developed more in the eleventh century, as we have discussed earlier. It survived and followed a different path, becoming mixed with the Tibetans' own Bonpo pagan concepts of black magic, sorcery and witchcraft. Tibetan Tantra involves the occult, the magical. Even in modern times these traditional rituals exist. The Oracles, a sort of witch doctor advisor to the high Lamas, were formerly part of the Tibetan state. Some still remain in Ladakh They still use the medium of dance and trance to delve deep into the occult for answers, and to define auspicious moments for celebrating, appeasement and to invoke higher powers.

In its most visual forms, we see Tantric images depicted in the ritual embrace of the deities and the dakinis. Tantric temples often show these deities as ferocious, gruesome demons. In a dark, mysterious chamber of the Potala Palace in Lhasa, there are tall, grotesque, monstrous demons looming and lurking, sending a spine-chilling wave through the imagination. The power of destruction is enough to make one run in terror.

Some Tantrics and Siddhis, those with miraculous powers, were said to be able to project their own consciouness into other beings. We are in the realms of the exoteric now. Within the astral universe, the cosmos filled with good and evil thoughts, playing with fire of this magnitude is indeed playing with the supernatural. Some Tibetans claim to have been able to leave their earthly bodies, experience these supernatural phenomena and return to their living bodies. Such people are known as a Delog. Then there are the she-devils, the lhamos and the bhutas, evil spirits, the dragons of Tibet and Bhutan.

Reincarnation is central to Tibetan Buddhism and here again we find a link to Tantra. Some Tantrics believe that the soul enters a human being or a human condition to achieve its divine purpose. This soul cannot be destroyed, but merely passes from one life to the next. We may never glimpse into our past lives, but perhaps in fleeting moments, through premonitions for example, these lives can manifest. Why then do we not reap the benefits of these earlier lives? We do benefit, but for greater understanding we need to be free of past ideas. Some Tantric meditation endeavours to find the truths of earlier existences.

Recently there has been an upsurge of interest in the more physical forms of Tantra. Tantric yoga and Tantric sex are used to shortcut these other methods of finding the desired state of enlightenment, the release from earthly sufferings. The embrace of the couple is both physical and spiritual. Its adherents believe it allows the combined energies to flow, to enable the souls to be taken on to a higher astral plane.

Did all these forms of religious practice come from Tibet and influence earlier beliefs in Nepal? Could the erotic figures on temples be ritual embraces, a vestige of Tibetan Tantra, or pagan shamanism?

44

Other Religions and Beliefs

Shamans and Jhankris

In many parts of rural Nepal we also find faith healers, witchcraft and animistic ideas. Some people also perform ancient shamanistic rituals, although these ideas are more prevalent in the hill villages than in the Kathmandu Valley. A Shaman priest is called a Jhankri in Nepal, and is much like the Tibetan Oracles who use trance to invoke spirits. Many of the rituals are Tantric in nature.

Christians, Muslims and Sikhs

There are also a small number of Christians, Muslims and Sikhs in Nepal.

In Conclusion

We find in the Kathmandu Valley a combination of ancient animistic ideas followed by early Buddhism from India. Then there is the influence of Tantra on Buddhism, including Vajrayana ideas. Hinduism, with its gods, deities and complex beliefs, infiltrated into the valley from India. Worship of the Hindu goddesses became prevalent.

Today the Hindu culture has become intertwined with various different forms of Buddhism, which came originally

Vajra Yogini, Sankhu

from India and then, in a new form, back south across the Himalayas from Tibet.

All these aspects contribute to the rich, abundant, diverse forms and manifestations of religious belief that we find in the Kathmandu Valley today.

Of course this is a fairly simplistic outline description, which in no way claims to be comprehensive.

CHAPTER FOUR
People of the Valley

In ancient times, the Kathmandu Valley region was known as Nepal; the words Nepal, Nepar and Newar are considered to have originated from one common word. The Newari ethnic group are the traditional inhabitants of the Kathmandu Valley, and it is believed that the early Newari were probably related to the Kiranti and Licchavi people. Nowadays the Newari probably number only about half the valley's population. In recent years many other peoples have migrated to the valley and to other cities to find work. Often individual groups colonise certain areas of the city. For many years the area of Jyatha, between Thamel and Kantipath/Asan, was home to Sherpas down from the hills, involved in trekking agencies and shops. People from the east, the Limbus, Rais and many Tamangs can be seen, as well as Magars, Gurungs and Manangis from central Nepal, and the western Dolpa from Dolpo.

The Newari language is within the Tibeto-Burman category and many Maithili north Indian words are now used in Newari. The Newari script is derived from the ancient Gupta script. Originally the Newari were Buddhist, but as influences from India grew in the Licchavi period and after, many Hindu practices were integrated into the religious activities, giving the wealth of cultural interaction we see today.

Newari Traditions

The following information is given as an insight into Newari traditions, many of which are rapidly being reformed in the quest for modernisation:
-
Housing

Traditional Newari houses were built close together, along cobbled streets and alleys, several storeys high with many framed and beautifully carved windows and doors. Sometimes they have verandahs, with the roofs made of tile or slate. Many old Newari-style houses have windows and window frames that are beautifully decorated with carvings. Door lintels, door flaps and roof struts are adorned with motifs of snakes, mythical deities, monsters and demons.

In a multi-storied house, the ground floor, being dark and cold, was used to keep the livestock, fodder, firewood etc. The first floor was used mainly for family living, and the next floor was used to store grain and food stocks. The uppermost floor was used as the kitchen, and also for the family place of worship (**puja** room). There are still numerous Newari-style houses in Bhaktapur, but elsewhere many have now been pulled down. Nowadays, when people build houses, they do not use traditional designs and decorations; they generally dislike the look of old houses because they reflect a lower status.

Social Structure

There were sixty-four castes within Newari society. The social and religious organisation of the Newari community is known as the **guthi**. Guthis deal with many aspects of communal life. They maintain temples, rest houses, bridges and roads, organise festivals, cremate the dead, conduct funerals and perform pujas. Some guthis help with entertainment, fellowship, companionship, friendly associations and other activities of common interest. Buddhist and Hindu Newari people can be part of the guthis, which still exercise some influence on Newari life.

At one time everybody of the tole, village, or area was a guthi member, and they were all obliged to pay monthly or yearly donations. The lands were an endowment of one or several families and, in due time, these lands became the property of the entire guthi membership. The Jyapu caste of Newari mostly cultivated the land themselves, while the rest of the Newari community lands were leased out to tenants who paid their rent to the person appointed by the guthi members. Using the income from this, they conducted worship of the various deities and arranged feasts and festivities.

The Newari have always been craftsmen, traders and artisans, with skills that have enabled them to build planned cities with impressive temples, shrines and palaces. Newari people live in close communities. Their houses are joined to each other, having a common wall on both sides, i.e. like terraced houses. The community is separated into smaller social units known as Toles and Bahals. Extended families populate these smaller social units. Previously higher caste and richer Newari people lived in the centre of the village. The lower caste and other people lived further out. The untouchable castes inhabited the boundaries. Even now, after the break-up of the extended family, people still live closely as a community. Society still retains many restrictions and old taboos. Newaris have a patriarchal society, where the head of the family household is the father, and men generally dominate social institutions. But since many worship female deities, it is possible that Newari society was once matriarchal.

Marriage

Married couples in Newari society avoid the paternal lineage. Marriages from the maternal side can occur only after a gap of at least seven generations. Today many sons and daughters choose their own partners, but marriages generally do not take place in the four months of Chaitra, Kartik, Kachala and Poush.

Previously any man could marry a woman of another caste, so long as it was equal to their caste and compatible with their social norms. But when a Newari woman married a man of equal caste but from a different tribe, a form of social boycott generally occurred; she was removed from the guthi. If a Newari man married a woman of another tribe, which was considered a lower and incompatible caste, then the woman would never be accepted into Newar society. Today we find widows remarrying, a practice previously disapproved of.

In traditional Newari communities, the groom does not accompany the janti, the wedding procession. Men and women of the groom's family, e.g. brothers, cousins, relatives, friends, and neighbours participate in the procession. The wedding procession party is entertained with sweets, dried fruits, betel nuts and cigarettes before leaving for the girl's house. When the wedding procession reaches there, betel nuts and spices are presented to eat. After eating, the participants of the janti leave, while the close relatives remain. The bride's family provide them with food and lodging.

When the groom brings his bride to his home later on, she is made to stand at the front door while a priest makes her pay homage to the **Kul Devta** (lineage deity) of the groom's house, as well as to Ganesh and other gods and goddesses. Next, the groom's mother or, in her absence, any respected woman who is equal to the groom's mother, makes the bride perform the ritual of washing the feet of the groom. Then the keys of the house are handed to her. The handing over of the house keys symbolises that the bride is accepted as one of the groom's family, and that she accepts the responsibilities towards her husband.

Later the couple is blessed and the feasting begins. When the bride and groom have finished eating, they are taken to a nearby shrine or bahal, where the groom pours vermilion powder on to the bride's hair parting. Four days after the marriage, in the evening, male relatives of the bride go to meet her at her new home. She is then invited to visit her maternal home, accompanied by her husband. After reaching his in-laws' home, the groom is introduced to the bride's entire family and **Duchakegu** is performed. In this ritual, the groom has to present ten unbroken betel nuts to each of them and perform **Dhog** (pay respect).

A Newari woman is not permitted to give birth at the home where she was born, as it is not considered auspicious. Birth pollution of the first child is observed for six days among Newar people. For second and later children, birth pollution is observed for only four days. **Navran** is the naming ceremony of a newborn child, when an astrologer gives the child a proper name. This ceremony is held after the purification day. Until then an aunt gives the child a nickname.

Newari Rituals

The **Pasni** ritual, which is still common, is the initial rice-feeding ceremony for a baby. It is performed when a baby boy is six to eight months old and a baby girl seven months old. For this ceremony, an uncle has to provide the necessary items and new clothes for his nephew or niece. During the ceremony, toys, grains of rice, brick, some mud, some gold ornaments, a book and a pen etc. are gathered. All these items are placed on a large tray and shown to the child. The child then looks at these items and touches one of them. It is believed that the item which the child touches will indicate his future profession. In Newari the Budo-jngko is a rice-feeding ceremony, performed mainly for aged Newari men and women. It is similar to that done for a child reaching the age of five or six months, and it is performed three times.

Some unique Newari rituals are still considered very important to them. One of them is **Bel Biwaha**, wood apple marriage. This practice is an initiation ceremony for young Newari girls. A girl has to be married to a bel, wood apple, before her first menstrual period, i.e. before puberty. The bel or wood apple is considered as immortal man. The fruit is selected from a healthy Belpatra tree, often found in the valley near Shiva temples. The age of puberty is generally fixed at fourteen for the boys and twelve for girls. This ceremony is performed mostly when girls reach the age of seven to nine years. A Brahmin or astrologer sets an auspicious date, after examining the girl's horoscope. Hindus worship these Belpatra trees, connecting the tree symbolically with the lingam. They believe that if a woman hugs the Belpatra tree, then her husband will be able to satisfy her sexual desire. Young unmarried women also hug the trees, so that they can get a talented husband of good character.

Bahara was a ceremony performed on girls after they had completed the Bel Biwaha ritual. It was completed before puberty, or her initial menstruation period. The girl had to be kept in a dark room without any sunlight penetration for eleven days. She was not permitted to look at the face of any man, even a close male relative. On the twelfth day, she was taken out of the dark room, bathed and blindfolded. As soon as the sun shone on the horizon, her blindfold was removed and she had to watch the sunrise. The Bahara was also done with a group of girls kept together in a dark room.

There were also initiation ceremonies performed for young Newari boys such as **Chudakarma**, **Karnavedh** and **Bratabandh**. Chudakarma is an initial hair-shaving ritual done by Hindu Newari people when their boys are five to seven years old. In this ritual, before shaving, the razor is worshipped by his father's sister's husband or by an aunt. Then the uncle uses the razor and starts shaving the boy's hair. Later a barber can take over and complete the shaving. This hair-shaving ritual does not exist for Buddhist Newari people.

At one time Buddhist Newars, like the Sakya caste, would take a dying person to the top floor of the house. After death the deceased person was brought downstairs and laid on a structure made of green bamboo. Then the deceased was taken to the riverbank. Other Newaris perform the death rites differently. For ordinary Newar people, a dying person is kept on the ground floor, which is dark and damp, or placed at a ritually purified spot. During the last moments his or her husband, wife or eldest son has to stay at his feet. The son has to pour water at his feet continuously until his death. After death has occurred, two oil lamps are lit and placed, one at the forehead and one at the feet of the deceased.

Because of this Newari people consider that lighting two oil lamps on any other occasion is inauspicious or a bad omen.

Both Hindu and Buddhist Newari people cremate all their dead, except for adults who die from epidemic disease or plague. These bodies are not cremated, but buried. Stillborn babies and those who die when less than three months old, not having performed any religious rituals, are also buried. The Kapil Newari do not cremate their deceased. They bury their deceased in a sitting posture, pour an amount of salt over the corpse according to their status, and then fill the grave.

Hindu Newaris observe a death 'pollution' for twelve days for their family's immediate members. On the thirteenth day, the family and the surroundings of the household are purified. If a death occurs at the birth home of a married woman, she has to observe death pollution for only four days at her home. During death pollution, Newari abstain from eating rice, curries, lentil, salt, oils and pickles.

This concludes our brief look at the traditions and the people of the valley. Today the population has exploded, with people from every ethnic group represented in the cities. The hectic pace of modern life in Kathmandu is a far cry from what it was less than twenty-five years ago.

The Sherpa Co-Operative 1979

The Sherpa Co-Operative was a trekking company founded by Mike Cheney, an ex-tea planter and plainly someone who would never return to the old country. He was 'staying on' and that was that. Purna was his trusted handyman and wheeler-dealer. Purna could sell anything. Both Purna and Mike were on the Chris Bonington Everest South West Face expedition that put Dougal Haston and Doug Scott on the summit. This was one of the last big expeditions to Everest.

The office of the Sherpa Co-Op was at Kamal Pokhari by the Krishna bakery, a building that still stands today in 2003. The office building was unpainted, stood in the grounds of a grassy yard and had a permanent smell of urine emanating from the toilet. One day a Brahmin bull came into the yard and decided to stay for a while. Another day famous mountaineers would be in to sort out their climbing Sherpas and porters.

Mike was always to be seen in long baggy khaki shorts and yellow jumper, come summer or winter. His mount was an ancient Indian Hero bicycle. He stood no nonsense and ran a good outfit. Rumours abounded that he had visited some regions of the country yet to be opened. He spoke the language fluently and, despite a hunched back, remained pleasant and helpful. He too spoke loudly in Nepali. Today the Sherpa Co-op yard is no more, buried under a mountain of concrete that is the Marco Polo Business Hotel. The Brahmin bull is no more. Most of the old cows that roamed about in Kathmandu have now taken to greener pastures. Even the packs of dogs have slunk away in disgust at the fumes.

Sadly too, both Mike and Purna have passed away. Of the other characters who worked at the Sherpa Co-

Op, one ran off with some funds and another runs a different travel company. One sirdar opened a trekkers' equipment shop in Jyatha, another married a Belgian lady, bought Russian helicopters and ran a trekking outfit. Another moved from trekking companies to travel companies. Some others returned to the Khumbu to open lodges. Others drank themselves into oblivion.

All in the rich tapestry of life in Kathmandu and Nepal.

Man in Valley

CHAPTER FIVE
Festivals

The festivals of Nepal are celebrated throughout the year in great profusion, and in an amazing riot of colour and enthusiasm. Most festivals coincide with the full moon each month, and as such follow a lunar calendar. Each month a different deity is worshipped. Most festivals reflect the Hindu/Buddhist mix, while others are purely one or the other. The Tibetan festival Losar is basically for Tibetans and Buddhists. Shivaratri is predominantly a Hindu festival.

April/May—Baisakh

The festive year begins with the Nepalese New Year. This is the beginning of the official Nepalese New Year. New Year is always mid-April and does not conform to the normal pattern connected to the lunar periods.

Bisket Jatra This festival is celebrated in Bhaktapur and Thimi, and is the most important New Year festival in the Kathmandu valley. The word "bisket" is derived from the Newari words "bi" for snake and "syako" for slaughter. The Malla Kings here gave their patronage to the festivities. The festival honours the Goddess Bhadrakali, who rides through the city accompanied by the image of Bhairab, the demonic destructive incarnate of Shiva, on a huge chariot with four massive wooden wheels. Each wheel is said to represent one of the four Vedas - ancient Indian scripts. Various celebrations take place all over the city including a riotous tug of war on New Years day. Later a wicker lamp procession parades to Dattatreya square and all these festivities continue for nine days.

Bal Kumari Jatra is another New Year festival celebrated in Thimi, a village 2 kilometres west of Bhaktapur. Bal Kumari, not to be confused with the living goddess Kumari, is yet another consort and female representation of Lord Bhairab. She has an ancient pagoda temple in the centre of Thimi, which is surrounded by worshippers bringing colourful gifts of flowers, fruits, vegetables, rice and coins. Ganesh, the elephant god, also plays an important part in this festival. Musicians play drums and clash cymbals wildly, as teams of men carry heavy khats (a small ornate enclosed box-like temple structure) on bamboo poles supported on their shoulders. The tiered brass roofs are brightly decorated and inside, the deities ride in style, long-fringed multi-coloured umbrellas perched high above. The festival concludes reluctantly after the gods go home.

Bode Tongue-boring Ceremony is a further New Year festival celebrated in the nearby village of Bode, at the Mahalakshmi temple. Usually one of the villagers volunteers for this. For four days before the festival, the man must eat only one sparse meal of ritually clean foods per day, and must shave all his bodily hair. No one must touch him, so he remains undefiled. The day before he must fast, while all visitors to the house must be offered food and drink. On the day itself, his tongue is pierced by a metal spike, and he walks around the village carrying a bamboo yoke of flaming torches for all to admire his penance. Back at the temple, the priest removes the needle, and fills the hole with mud from the floor, thought to have healing properties. If no blood has been shed, he is regarded as having earned so much merit that he will go straight to heaven, avoiding the endless cycle of rebirth.

Mata Tirtha Puja (Mothers' Day) is celebrated on the last day of the dark fortnight of Baisakh. This is the day when all people make a special effort to go to their mother's home, laden with gifts and specially prepared foods. If their mother is dead, they make a pilgrimage to Mata Tirtha, a site six miles southwest of Kathmandu, near the Machha Narayan temple. Here are two ponds. One is for bathing in; the other smaller one is where the reflection of one's mother's face is said to be seen. Here gifts of sweetmeats, foods and red powder are presented to the gods. Sometimes small clay dishes with lighted oil wicks are left to float on the pond in their mother's memory.

Rato Machhendranath

Rato Machhendranath chariot

Rato Machhendranath Jatra is one of the most colourful and elaborate
festivals of the whole valley. It takes place in Patan and is one of the main
festivals of the valley. Machhendranath appears in red and white form and
each aspect is assumed to be the same god. Buddhists consider the god to
be Padmapani, the fourth disciple of the Buddha, also known as
Avalokiteshvara or Lokeshvara. Hindus worship Machhendranath as the
compassionate god of mercy, Karunamaya. There are many legends linked
to Machhendranath. The name itself emanates from the word Machha,
meaning fish in Newari. One legend about Machhendranath concerns his
birth. It was said that a Brahmin woman gave birth to a son on an inauspicious day. So forbidding were all the astrological signs that the baby was
cast into the sea. But a great fish came by and swallowed the baby and
nurtured it. When Shiva heard this tale he released the child, who hence-
forth became known as Lord Machhendranath.

At different seasons of the year the idol of the Red Machhendranath
is found residing in either Bungamati or the Ta Bahal in Patan. The idol has
a ceremonial bathing and repainting some weeks before the festival. In late
April or early May the red five-foot image of Machhendranath is placed
on a chariot with large wooden wheels. The wheels represent the Bhairabs
who helped to carry Machhendranath from Assam to Kathmandu. He
must be appeased, for he is a demonic god. Above this is a massive
platform with a gilded temple housing the idol. A fifty-foot spire of wood
covered in green branches with red flags and drapes is placed above the
idol. At the front is a massive wooden beam structure which has Karkot,
the snake demon's image, attached to it. Originally men from nearby Kirtipur
pulled this massive unwieldy structure, but nowadays any able-bodied
person seems to help. A smaller chariot follows, containing the idol of Min
Nath, also called Chakwa Dev.

The two chariots are pulled very slowly each day through the suburbs of Patan, from Pulchowk to Gabahal and on to Sundhara, where they
rest for a few days. Then they proceed to Lagankhel, where they circle the
tree representing the mother of Machhendranath. Here the dropping of
some auspicious items occurs, in particular the coconut ceremony, where
a coconut is thrown down into the attentive crowd below; he who catches
the coconut will have a son. Finally they lumber on towards Jawalakhel; it
may take a month in all to reach there. On an auspicious date later, the
climax of the festival concludes with Bhoto Jatra, when a sacred waistcoat
is displayed for all to see, including the King and Queen and Kumari of
Patan. Afterwards the idol of the red Machhendranath, the god of rain and

good harvest, returns to his resident temple in Bungamati, a village south of Patan.

Every twelve years (2003 was one of these years) the festival is more elaborate and takes longer. The idol is bathed in Bungamati and the rath or chariot is assembled there. Then the chariot is pulled from Bungamati to Patan. After the usual activities in Patan, the chariot is then pulled to the Nakhu River, where a ritual meeting of the snake couple is said to take place. Afterwards the idol and its chariot continue back to Bungamati. The Bhoto Jatra then takes place here instead of in Patan. On this year the idol spends more of the preceding winter in Bungamati.

Percy Brown visited the valley in 1912 and describes the Rato Machhendranath festival as follows: -

The car (chariot) is a huge, unwieldy structure with massive wheels, on the solid spokes of which are painted in distinctive colours the eyes of Bhairab or Shiva. Surmounting this is a chamber containing the deity, built up in the form of a column, somewhat resembling a maypole, and between 60 and 70 feet high. This construction is dragged for a mile and a half, but this short journey ordinarily occupies at least four days, as certain prescribed halts are made, and neither is the car itself nor are the roads adapted for easy progression. The scene is a wild and barbaric one. Through the narrow streets overhung by wooden balconies crammed with excited groups of onlookers, or across the great open square, the platforms of all the picturesque buildings forming vantage grounds on which the crowds congregate, the car, dragged by over a hundred willing devotees, makes its triumphal tour...

The superstructure of the car, overlaid with plates of copper-gilt, and surmounted by a metal umbrella with gay streamers and ribbons, sways until it almost

> *overturns as the groaning wheels bump over the uneven pavement of the city, or sink deep into the soft soil of the roadway outside. Willing hands cling manfully to the guide ropes, and thus accident is averted. Like a great ship staggering through a heavy sea...*
>
> *A procession naturally accompanies the car, elephants gaily painted and caparisoned move ponderously along, bearing their gold and silver howdahs the royalties of the state. Bands make joyful, if somewhat barbaric, music on tambourines, cymbals, trumpets, conches and drums, while bevies of girls carrying garlands of flowers enliven the proceedings with song and dance. Other attendants carry great bells on poles, golden umbrellas, incense burners, fly whisks, banners and all the insignia of the great deity...*

Very little has changed since that time. Electric cables have to be removed now, and the houses are taller, but the great chariot still lumbers along, often at an alarming angle. Bands and groups of musicians accompany the idol, whose strange but serene expression is unchanging throughout.

Buddha Jayanti is celebrated on the full moon, when the houses and stupas at Swayambhunath, in particular, as well as at Boudhanath and Chabahil, are decorated with flags. Butter lamps and lights illuminate the stupa at Swayambhunath. At Boudhanath an elephant sometimes carries the image of Buddha around the great shrine, with the lamas chanting. The festival celebrates the birth of Buddha, his enlightenment and death. Festivities also take place in the three cities of the valley.

May/June—Jestha

Avalokiteshvara Jatra is a small celebration that takes place in Thimi. The red-faced idol is known locally as Padmapani Lokeshvara and is bathed, repainted and paraded within the city for a week.

Kumar Sasthi celebrates the god Kumar and occurs at the start of the rice-planting season. This is also the time to clean wells and dig out water channels, thus removing snake demons. Kumar is the warrior god, a son of Shiva. Legend has it that when demons vanquished Indra from his throne, Vishnu declared that nothing would happen until a son was born of Shiva and Parvati. The god of fire, Agni, disguised as a beggar, was sent to Shiva's palace on Mount Kailash in Tibet. But Agni interrupted the lovemaking of Shiva and his consort. Shiva was furious at this disturbance, but as he was about to send flames from his third eye to destroy Agni, Parvati intervened. Shiva, in anger, ejected his semen into the beggar's hand, and he swallowed it. Then, engulfed with burning, Agni vomited the semen out and into the river Ganges, whereupon a son known as Kumar was born. Kumar annihilated the demons, and Indra was reinstalled. A red circle traced on the ground usually represents Kumar. Human sacrifice once accompanied this festival, in particular at the Kankeshwari temple. Kumar resides in the temple of Jaisidewal in the old city where much of the action takes place.

July/August—Shravan

During this month very few festivals are held — it is considered a time of illness and deprivation, and most of the gods go away for the season. But man still faces problems at this time, and the following festival illustrates one such story.

Ghanta Karna is the most dreadful of demons opposing Vishnu. The festival celebrates the night of the wicked ones and takes place during the monsoon, on the fourteenth day of the dark fortnight. A man from one of the lowly castes represents the demon. Virtually naked and covered in lurid sexual depictions, he is cheered and booed in the streets, but begs for coins. No one wishing to avoid the wrath of the demon fails to place a coin. Later he is tied to a bamboo frame, which is then set alight. The man escapes at the last minute, still with the coins, and the demon is vanquished.

August/September—Bhadra

The sacred month of **Gunla** is dedicated to the Lord Buddha, with worship taking place throughout the valley, but in particular at Swayambhunath.

Gunla is celebrated by the Newari Buddhists of the valley. Devotees visit many of the valley's significant shrines; some will involve long walks. Each day during Gunla Buddhist women make deities or rice flour or clay, and at the end all these idols are immersed in holy waters. Many women fast to draw themselves towards enlightenment.

Naga Panchami is celebrated during the rainy season, and is a festival during which snakes and serpents are worshipped. Although generally unseen, snakes are quite common, but in any case the people seek to appease the serpent spirits in order to avoid mishaps. There are many legends and stories about snakes in the rich tapestry of the folklore of the valley. One is particularly amusing: —

Once upon a time a wicked snake dwelt in the Sidha Pokhari pond near Bhaktapur. One day a Tantric holy man came by with his companion to rid the pond of the snake. He said to his companion, "I will go into the pond as a serpent. If the snake kills me you will see milk rising; if I kill the snake you will see blood. Then you must throw over some holy rice to restore me to human form." When blood surfaced his companion, in shock and fear, forgot the rice and ran to Thimi for help, but it was too late. The Tantric holy man remained as a serpent, and is still living in the lake. People still prefer to avoid the pond in Bhaktapur.

Janai Purni is celebrated at full moon, when the Brahman and Chettri castes exchange the Janai or sacred thread. This represents a ceremonial exchange of ideas. The festival is celebrated in Patan at the Kumbheshwar Mahadev temple. Here a Shiva lingam phallus is erected in a pool. Water is then believed to flow from the sacred lake at Gosainkund, on a ridge near Langtang north of Kathmandu, to the pool in Patan. Pilgrims flock to the Gosainkund Lake to worship Shiva in a gathering or mela. The pilgrimage is arduous, as it takes place during the full fury of the monsoon.

Gai Jatra is the cow festival, on the day following Janai Purni, when people pay homage to holy cows. Cows, it is said, help with the difficult passage to the next world. This festival is particularly important to families who have had a recent bereavement. A procession of bands and deco-rated cows makes its way through the streets, passing Hanuman Dhoka in Kathmandu. Similar activities take place elsewhere. Men dress like women and monsters, and everyone pokes fun at celebrities, politicians and other well-known personalities. Gai Jatra is a colourful affair throughout the valley. Some of the most spectacular festivities occur in Bhaktapur.

Krishna Jyanti Krishna is a popular god, being an example to all the men of the valley. This day celebrates his birthday. He is regarded as the ideal example of manhood. Devotion to him promises salvation to those who act unselfishly on earth. As an incarnation of Vishnu, he ensures the eventual victory of goodness over evil in men's souls. His fun-loving romantic adventures with the cowgirls, the gopis, are well known, as is his flute playing. Images of Krishna appear everywhere. He is worshipped in Patan at the Krishna temple. Wherever vice appears, Krishna will come forth to save the righteous and punish the evil.

Gokarna Aunsi (Fathers' Day) is when fathers are revered and given offerings. It is of particular importance to the sons of fathers recently passed away. It takes place when the moon is dark. Many people travel to Gokarna, east of Pashupatinath, some way beyond Boudhanath. Here at the shrine of Gokarneswar Mahadev, people gather to pay homage to the Shiva lingam, which is in close contact with the dead souls. As on mothers' day, people whose fathers are living go to their homes, laden with gifts and sweetmeats, for family feasts and celebrations.

Teej Brata is a festival celebrated only by women. After a large feast, they begin a twenty-four hour period of complete fasting to cleanse their souls and hope for a happy future. The women of the valley go to Pashupatinath to offer puja to Shiva and his consort, Parvati. The flame of an oil lamp must remain alight throughout the night for good omens. Next morning the women must bring food gifts to their husbands and bathe in holy waters.

Ganesh Chata takes place on the fourth day of the bright fortnight, during the women's Teej festival, and is held in honour of the elephant god Ganesh. Ganesh is worshipped as the god of good luck and success. No ceremony or venture of any kind can commence until Ganesh has been worshipped. Shrines devoted to him are to be seen in most neighbourhoods. According to legend, the moon once offended Ganesh, and as a result he cursed her, saying that anyone who set eyes on her would become a thief. So she disappeared from the world. But the other gods begged him to let her come back to lighten their darkness. He agreed, on condition that the curse would remain effective on one day only. So on the night of this festival people remain inside, to avoid seeing the moon. It is a good night for thieves, for if they succeed it bodes well for their future career as a thief!

Indra Jatra is celebrated for eight days and is a happy occasion. It celebrates the capture of the god Indra when he came to the valley in disguise. Once the people realised that Indra was among them, they rejoiced and paid homage. A flagpole is erected at the Royal Palace and this represents the presence of the god Indra. This pole is selected by chance using a sacrificial goat from the forest near Bhaktapur. The huge image of Seto Bhairab in the Kathmandu Durbar Square is unveiled and at different times sacred rice beer flows from his mouth for the joy of the devotees. Various plays are performed, and elephants are paraded. Masked dancing and other dances also take place. In one dance a long-haired blue Bhairab and two companions perform for the happy crowd. The demon god Bhairab is worshipped throughout the city. On the full moon the Kumari living goddess joins in the festivities. On this day she gives Tika to the King and all hope for another auspicious year. This is perhaps the most auspicious ceremony of the festival. Bhairab, Ganesh and the Kumari ride in chariots around the streets of old Kathmandu, taking different routes. The festival concludes down by the river Bagmati, at the shrine of Pachali Bhairab near Teku.

September/October—Aswin

Dashain celebrates the forces of good over evil, and is an exuberant almost two-week-long festival. It is a celebration of the victory of Rama over the demon Ravena, a story told in the Ramayana epic. This is a hugely significant festival for families, whose members travel enormous distances in order to be united in their family homes. Houses are cleansed and the goddess Durga is worshipped; some rituals are Tantric in nature. The goddess Durga is represented as a vessel filled with holy water. The eighth night is Kali Ratri, when hundreds of buffaloes, goats, sheep, chickens and ducks are sacrificed. On the ninth day goats and buffaloes are sacrificed to Durga and the blood is used ritually to bless all moving vehicles. Even aircraft receive a blood blessing. The military perform a sacrificial slaughter of many animals in the Kot Square near Hanuman Dhoka. Dashain is celebrated throughout the valley and all over the country. In

Patan the Astha Matrika dances are performed along with other parades and celebrations. The Kumari of Bhaktapur appears at this time and is carried to the Taleju temple each morning. The tenth and concluding day witnesses the offering of tika, blessings within family groups, as well as some public shamanistic, tantric trance rituals.

Pachali Bhairav is also celebrated during Dashain by some castes. Pachali Bhairab is worshipped in Teku. Bhairab, Shiva in demon form, is one of the most commonly worshipped gods in Nepal. Animal sacrifices take place at the shrine, as well as at the image of Bhairab in Kathmandu Durbar Square. Ganesh and the Kumari are part of the festivities.

October/November —Kartik

Tihar/Diwali is a pleasant festival without gruesome sacrifices. It is the festival of lights and Lakshmi Puja, worshipping the goddess of wealth, the wife of Vishnu. This is also the time to give offerings to Yama, god of death. On different days crows, dogs and cows are also worshipped, with bright garlands of marigolds around their necks and red tikas on their foreheads, if they get close enough! On the last day, Bhai Tika, sisters give offerings to their brothers. Lights shine everywhere and at the doorway of each house is a butter lamp and offerings of rice.

Haribodhini Ekadasi celebrates the return of Vishnu from the underworld. Along the river south of the old Kathmandu, the sun god Surya and Narayan are worshipped. They both offer life and light, watching over good and evil in beings. Narayan is also Vishnu. Offerings take place at Changu Narayan temple north of Bhaktapur, not far from Nagarkot. The idol of the sleeping Vishnu at Budhanilkantha becomes the focus of the offerings. It is said that the great idol was once buried under a landslide from Shivapuri hill and rediscovered by farmers tilling the land nearby. Many tales abound about the origins of this idol.

November/December —Mangsir

Gujeshwari Jatra is a lesser-known festival that takes place just northeast of Pashupatinath at the temple dedicated to Gujeshwari, where there is a small sacred water hole. It is here that the lotus from Swayambhunath is said to have come to rest. Gujeshwari is another manifestation of Kali,

Durga and Taleju, the fearsome aspects of Shiva's consort Parvati. She represents the Shakti or female aspect. A vessel of water is carried from the Kathmandu Taleju temple to Gujeshwari. Its journey continues from the temple through Pashupatinath and back to the great Taleju temple once more.

Indrayani Puja is a rather strange Tantric festival which takes place on the Vishnumati river. Indrayani is also known as Luti Ajima, a powerful grandmother goddess who must be appeased by blood sacrifices to ward off disease. During the celebration a buffalo is sacrificed. Its head is tossed into a fire to appease the god of fire, Agni. Other animals such as snakes were once sacrificed to the fire god. Celebrations take place at Thahiti Square with musicians playing, and at Kirtipur, see below.

Bakhu Mara Asthami is celebrated in Kirtipur for three days. It is known as the pigeon festival and is a celebration of Indrayani. The pigeons were once part of the main Indrayani sacrifices. The image of the goddess is paraded in a khat from the Bagh Bhairab temple and taken beyond the city limits, where it rests before returning to Bagh Bhairab. A royal sword representing the monarch is presented to the goddess and various rites are performed.

Bala Chaturdasi is a rather strange festival that remembers Bala, a man who became a demon by accident. It is celebrated at Pashupatinath, where grains are offered in worship. There are many tales concerning Bala; most say that Bala became a demon by unwittingly eating the flesh from a cremated body at the ghats. Bala was made drunk and killed.

Mani Rimdu is celebrated by Sherpa people in the valley. However the main festivities take place in the region of Solu Khumbu at Thyangboche and Thame near Namche Bazaar. It is a lively, colourful Buddhist festival with masked dancing and comic role-playing, and marks the emergence of Buddhist doctrine over the animistic Bonpo religion that predated it in Tibet.

Dhanya Purnima is a festival mainly celebrated by the valley farmers. It is a very old tradition and takes place after the harvest on full moon in December. People make yomarhi cakes and offer then around. A legend recounts that Kubera, god of wealth, came disguised as a beggar to a house in Panauti and was given some yomarhi cakes, and so the festival began.

December/January—Poush

At this time of year when it is cold no festivals take place, as it is considered inauspicious.

Seto Machhendranath bathing. The first preparations of this great festival take place now, but the actual festival of Seto Machhendranath is three months later. The ritual bathing of the idol takes place amidst song, music and worship. The Kumari is also present.

January/February—Magh

Magh Sankranti marks the end of cold inauspicious winter months and is the awakening month for religious life. It is an auspicious time for marriage and is when most weddings are held. At this time Saraswati, the goddess of learning and knowledge, is worshipped at a shrine at Swayambhunath.

Losar is celebrated by the Tibetan community and marks the Tibetan New Year. Parades and processions take place at all the Buddhist stupas, but Boudhanath is the main centre of activity. Here the monks parade around the stupa carrying an image of the Dalai Lama. Horns are blown loudly and people throw Tsampa, roasted barley.

The Festival of Lights is also celebrated at Boudhanath, on the night of the full moon of Magh. Tibetans and Buddhist people from the northern mountains, as well as from Sikkim and Bhutan, come to the shrine. The head lama, who represents the Dalai Lama, performs elaborate rituals before the image of Tasca Muni, a Tibetan goddess who is a tantric image of the terrifying goddess, Kali.

Mila Punhi is another one-day festival celebrated on the full moon of Magh. According to legend, Narayan decided to leave Changu for Benares, but when he came to bid farewell to the king at Hanuman Dhoka, the king tried to dissuade him from leaving the valley. Narayan decided to go anyway, but when hundreds of clay pots inexplicably exploded, he decided to stay at Changu after all. During this festival, a procession leaves Changu in the morning, carrying Narayan in his khat all the way to Kathmandu. They pass through the old city and meet the Kumari goddess at the Taleju temple. When Narayan leaves the Taleju temple, children break clay pots in celebration of the old legend, and Narayan returns to Changu Narayan overnight.

February/March—Falgun

Shiva Ratri is one of the most important festivals in the Kathmandu Valley, taking place again at Pashupatinath. It is celebrated as the birthday of Shiva at new moon in the Nepali month of Falgun, with thousands of devotees bathing in the Bagmati River and offering puja to the Shiva lingams. Hundreds of holy men, sadhus and sages converge on the site and smoke *ganga*, the intoxicant of Shiva. Shiva has many aspects, not all destructive; he is Nataraj the dancing Shiva, he is Mahadev, gracious and supreme. He is worshipped as the god of reproduction, hence the lingams and yonis that are seen in such profusion at Pashupatinath and elsewhere. The festival involves fasting and then comes the night (*ratri*) of Shiva, when the flames of campfires flicker, and people worship throughout the hours of darkness.

Holi is a very boisterous and colourful affair, characterised by the traditional throwing of coloured dyes at all that pass by. It is celebrated in remembrance of the demon Holika. A pole, the chir, is erected for the duration of the celebration and is burnt at the end. Fire was said to have destroyed the demon Holika. Young men brazenly approach young girls, emboldened by the spirit of the festival. It is definitely not a good idea to wear any valuable clothing on this day!

In addition to the normal festivities, a special Tantric ritual sacrifice of a buffalo is carried out at Itum Bahal and beside the Vishnumati River. This ritual is to appease the child-eating ogre, Guru Mapa. His image is to be seen in Itum Bahal.

Shiva Ratri, spring 1982

We cycle out of Thamel and head for Pashupatinath.
Thousands of people are converging on the holy shrine,
for this is to be the night of Shiva, when devotees and

---

pilgrims gather to pay homage to Lord Shiva. Shiva is the most prominent god of the valley. As lord of destruction he must be appeased, or death and despair will follow. We pass women dressed in their finest silk saris. Every colour of the rainbow is displayed; red is the dominant colour. The men too are in their finest clothes, some traditional, others in pilgrims' cotton dhotis, sarong-style. Sadhus have congregated at the riverside, smoking the ganga weed and smeared in ash or vermilion powder.

As the hot sun moves westward, heavy clouds are building. A thick haze obscures the hills on the rim of the valley. At dusk the lights of a thousand fires cast shadows under the craggy trees of the deer forest. Voices echo around the shrines. The crowds are intense. Pilgrims wash and musicians play haunting melodies. Some chant holy praises of Mahadev, others cry out the praises of Pashupati. In the crush of the crowd, the smell of hot bodies is dominant; the air is filled with the smell of hashish, bidis – local rolled tobacco-leaf cigarettes, incense and perfume.

An intoxicating vision is before us, Lord Shiva has arrived. Lord Shiva is touching Pashupatinath tonight.

Chakandeo Jatra is a festival centred on the Thamel Bahal temple, and it relates to a merchant, Singha Sarastra Bahu, who travelled to Tibet. According to legends, many of his accompanying traders fell in with maidens who were, in reality, demons. The god of mercy Machhendranath revealed the nature of the maidens to Singha, so all decided to return to Kathmandu. A flying white horse was sent to bring them home to Kathmandu, but only on condition that they did not look back. Many of the merchants perished when they could not resist just one last glance at the beautiful maiden devils, but Singha was saved, as he did not yield to this temptation. Some of the demon maidens came to Kathmandu; many perished but Singha saved the day. Singha ruled Thamel with great wisdom and became known as Chakandeo. The idol of Chakandeo is paraded around the old city on the full moon of March and is worshipped to give wisdom.

March/April—Chaitra

Adinath Jatra takes place at Chobar. The festival lasts nine days and is celebrated by the Newari Buddhists of the valley who revere Adinath as Lokeshvara at Chobar. Adinath is also linked to Manjushri who, in legend, cut through the gorge here to drain the great lake of the valley. Other Lokeshvara temples are at Patan, Bungamati, Nala and the Jan Bahal in Asan. The image is ritually bathed in the river below the hill and after some days it returns in a khat to its home on the hill.

Pisach Chaturdasi The pisach are a multitude of evil spirits that bring disease. At this hot time of year, even Shiva is in hiding. His lingam is found in unclean places. On this day the valley is cleaned and Shiva once again protects. Mustard flowers and radishes are offered to the unseen god. The Ajima grandmother goddesses are worshipped. Bhadrakali, being one, is shown particular devotion. Masked dancers perform at Naradevi in old Kathmandu. Pahachare is also a celebration at this time.

Ghora Jatra takes place on the central Tundikhel field, and nowadays is a parade of horsemanship. Ghore means horse.

Balaju Jatra is a celebration that culminates in ritual cleansing and holy bathing at the Balaju water gardens. The sleeping or reclining Vishnu is worshipped here. Buddhists make offerings at Swayambhunath.

Chaitra Dashain is a small celebration, offering homage to Durga exactly six months before the main Dashain festival. People make offerings at the various Bhagawati temples and ritual animal sacrifices also take place at Hanuman Dhoka.

Seto Machhendranath Jatra Like his red (Rato) counterpart in Patan, Seto Machhendranath is believed to be an incarnate of Avalokiteshvara, a Buddhist disciple or bodhisattva. Hindus worship the white (Seto) Machhendranath, for he gives longevity and fertility to women. Hindus also fete him as the compassionate God of Mercy, Karunamaya.

A legend about the Seto Machhendranath idol tells how when a king invaded the valley, he had the idol taken away. It became neglected and was tossed into the Gandaki River. But the king became ill and had it retrieved and taken to Kathmandu. Again it was discarded and became buried. A Newari porter finally found it at Jamal, near Rani Pokhari, and thus the idol was saved and placed in a temple nearby in Asan Tole. The temple is now to be found in the heart of the old city bazaars of Asan.

The procession takes place in March/April, when the idol is placed between its Buddhist attendants, the green and white Taras, and rides through the streets of Kathmandu on a towering chariot. The chariot is assembled at Jamal. The Newari priests take the idol of the White Machhendranath from Jan Bahal in a khat via Indrachowk to rendezvous with the chariot. Meanwhile the Kumari is carried to the Taleju temple for sacred rituals. The journey of the idol will take at least three days and will generally provide some tense moments, as the great chariot inches its way along the narrow streets and over rough lanes. The chariot goes via Asan to Hanuman Dhoka and then south to Lagan. Here, as in Patan, it circles the sacred tree before the festivities conclude. The idol later returns to its home in the Jan Bahal.

Sankhu Jatra takes place at the Gum Bahal shrine of Vajra Yogini. Hindus regard the Yogini as a source of energy, while Buddhists revere her as a source of wisdom. Vajra Yogini is sometimes known as Khadga Yogini here. The idol is carried in a khat down to Sankhu, and then returned to her shrine during the celebrations.

Sapana Tirtha Mela is the last festival of the Newari year and also marks the end of the year. Its origins again reside in legends, but the focal point of the action is a pond near Tokha village, north of the modern ring road below the Shivapuri hills. This is the place of holy dreams. One of the stories relates that a princess married a leper after her father the King, in jest, said she would not be wealthy but poor. The King disowned his daughter when she married the leper. In destitution, one day she had a dream. On the eve of the New Year she took her husband to the pond at Tokha and he was miraculously cured, becoming a handsome prince.

Pilgrims begin their homage at the source of the Bagmati in the hills to the north. Then they go to a cave on Vishnu Nab hill and also the source of the Vishnumati River, before coming to Tokha.

The descriptions of the festivals of the valley are necessarily brief in this book; a detailed description would fill all the pages and more. But even within these short depictions, one can pick out many of the places where the celebrations occur. There are innumerable shrines, temples and palaces to see; every corner hides an unexpected treasure.

CHAPTER SIX
Art of the Kathmandu Valley

There are many forms of art throughout the valley. Some are quite shocking! In terms of erotic art, there are basically two forms. There is the simple art in stone and the art that is carved in wood. There is also the rather rare erotic art of paintings and tangkas. Other art involves those forms made by skilled artisans, such as carpet making, weaving, pottery, rice paper making, painting of pictures, mandalas etc, wood carving, stone carving, brass and copper wares, idol products and many others.

The lotus flower often appears in close connection with some of the erotic art. It is also seen as a plinth or base for other art forms showing the gods and deities. The lotus plant is a link for Buddhists to the world of erotic art. It represents the lingam. It is at the heart of the creation of life. Brahma, the creator, is born of a lotus flower. The lotus is pure and from it life will spring. The lotus is depicted with erotic art almost as an antidote to the images themselves.

Throughout the valley we see amazing bronze and gilded work. The bronze is a particular skill of the Newari. The centres for this art form are Patan and also Bhojpur in the East of Nepal. The method used is called the lost wax method. In this method wax is used to outline the image, then covered with clay. After heating the wax is drained and the molten metal is poured in afterwards. See book list for more information.

Temple Art Forms and most common features

At every turn in the streets of the valley one will find temples and shrines. The visual impression is one of overload. Yet there is some order in the singularly disordered. Buddha images are numbered in the thousands. Yet each temple is defined by the idols within its precincts; the Buddhas relate to the merits desired. The idols of the gods define the emotions, the desires, and the needs of the worshippers. We can never describe the meaning of each image or its position in the temple hierarchy, but the main to look for are described below.

Torana is the entrance plate above the door to the temple, often semi-circular and in gold or gilded metal. It will depict the gods, often the deity inside the temple, as well as their vehicles and escorts. The fish-like, demonic-looking figures on many toranas are the deities' protectors. They are called Makara and often have trunk-like mouths. A birdman, Garuda, Chhepu or Kirtimukha figure usually sits above all the other images.

Pataka is a metal strip hanging down from the top of the temple, with a decoration at its base, a guide for the gods to descend to earth.

Gajura is the top part of a temple and is normally bell-shaped.

Pataka

Torana above Sun Dhoka gate, Bhaktapur

Temple Art and Architecture

Nearly all the significant temples of the valley are the tiered **'Dega'** style that is not strictly the same as the pagoda. The Dega style is not Chinese, but is more akin to some south Indian and Gupta period structures.

The **Dega** temples were constructed of brick, often glazed, and wood. The wood used was a type of teak (Sal). Gilded copper was used for roofing and decoration. Many adornments are in wood, gilded copper and bronze. Copper was the favourite metal of Newari craftsmen, partly due to the abundance of the raw materials in Nepal, but also because it was more easily worked. Newari craftsmen were in great demand and found in significant numbers in Tibet.

The oldest temple is at Panauti, just outside the valley to the east. It dates from 1294. Further multi-tiered versions appeared later, when the Taleju Mandir of the Kathmandu Durbar Square was constructed in 1564. Later more levels were added as construction techniques improved, culminating in the four tiers at Nala and Harisiddhi. Then the five tiers of Kumbeshwar in Patan and the Nyatapola of Bhaktapur, built in 1702, were constructed.

The less common tiered rectangular temples seen in the valley are often devoted to Bhairab. They have fewer openings, perhaps to keep the ferocious god inside!

Also rectangular are the Bhimsen temples, which invariably have the deity on the first floor. This also allows more congregating space below for meetings or, more commonly, for the merchants who worship Bhimsen.

Pitha means seat. These pitha-style temples have open ground floors with one wall at the back, and the other three sides open. Examples are Bal Kumari outside Patan, Vajra Varahi near Chapagaon, the Brahmayani temple in Thecho, and in Kathmandu the Kankeshwari temple. This style dates from 1600-1700 AD.

Also in the 17th century some **octagonal** temples were constructed, notably in the Royal Palace chowks of Kathmandu and Patan and also in the Kathmandu Durbar Square is the Krishna temple.

The **Mandapa**-style temples and structures have a large (and small) open pillared ground floor area that serves as a meeting area. The prime example is the famous Kasthamandap temple of Kathmandu, where the Gorakhnath idol is found in the centre. The Dattatreya temple in Bhaktapur was first constructed like this, before being modified. In Patan there are two small Mandapas north of the main Palace.

Dyochhen is a Tantric temple or meeting hall. Temples devoted to the Astha Matrikas are often in the Dyochhen style. Some small Dyochhens are like elaborate highly decorated houses with deities and even carvings, others are more open.

Other Structures

The Shikhara-style has two forms. The large ones, usually built in stone, are sometimes tiered, with each higher level occupying a smaller surface area. Pillars are common and the whole structure is built to look like a mountain, the home of the gods. The best example is the Krishna temple in Patan. The other types of shikhara shrines are the solid, tall but slimmer four-sided structures, often built in brick and plastered. Examples are seen at Swayambhu. The Rato Machhendranath temple in Bungamati has both pillars and a central solid tower.

Bahal is the communal enclosed courtyard that serves as a living place in the cities. A central chaitya will be found in most.

Bahi is a similar compound, but is used primarily for celibate monks and has long dormitory-style rooms on the first floor. The side quadrangle of Itum Bahal in Kathmandu has one such dormitory.

Bahal Bahi is a combination of the two above, for example the renovated I Baha Bahi in Patan.

Pathi is a rest house, which from a distance could be mistaken for a small temple, and indeed, often there is a shrine nearby. Thamel was on the edge of town on several important trade routes, and, before hotels existed, merchants would lie down to sleep at the pathi on the corner, where nowadays traders sell khukri knives and jewellery in the open.

Erotic Stone Carvings

In different parts of the valley we see extremely clear indications of simple erotic themes. Of course to the casual eye some of these might easily be misunderstood. Others are far more explicit, and appeal in these forms to the basic human instincts.

At Pashupatinath we witness the passing of the dead into the next life by fire. We also see many hundreds of what might be termed erotic carvings, statues and stone designs. These very simple depictions of creativity are the stone phalluses and circular saucepan-shaped platforms, representing the male and female life-giving organs. They are called the lingam and the yoni. The most popular image in Shaivism (Shiva worship) is that of the lingam, and it is often seen erected on an image representing the yoni. This is the sacred symbol of creation, and has been worshipped as such for thousands of years by millions of people. A lingam that has four faces around it is called the Chaturmukha version.

It is Shiva that is most revered in Nepal. Shiva can be appeased by worship, and can be pacified to perform great acts of creativity. Shiva is the one who can give new life, hence the connection with creation in all its forms. Shiva, by being the destroyer of evil, may also be considered the creator of happiness and peace. Shaivism is a very old religious tradition, having been present in India long before the entry of the Aryans and the development of Hinduism several thousand years ago. Images of Shiva lingams have been found in the early Indus civilisations of present-day Pakistan at Harappa and Mohenjodaro.

It is not hard to see the association of the human life-giving organs with the beliefs of creation and Shiva worship. Whether one can say they are erotic is another matter. They are there to give offerings and appeasement to the gods. Many are housed in chaityas, small stone temples. Further up the hill, past the viewing area at Pashupatinath, are several newly-renovated chaityas and a walkway.

These chaityas are square-shaped box shrines with a lingam or deity within, and are Hindu versions. A Buddhist chaitya is a small square-shaped shrine, usually with the four Dhyani or directional Buddhas capped by a small stupa. These Buddhas represent the cardinal directions of the universe and are found around stupas in small chapels.

When did the lingam-yoni stone depictions first originate? It is generally accepted that they first appeared in the Kathmandu Valley during the Licchavi period. That is believed to be in the period from 400 to 750 AD. The lingam and the yoni are not merely symbolic in the Hindu culture, but have developed into other religious concepts. In Nepal and India the Hindu influence has penetrated into Buddhist ideas. This might seem quite strange, because Buddhism is concerned more with the way life should be conducted, rather than the business of offering to a superior being, a god. However Buddhism has adapted to many influences, and none more so than in Nepal, as we have seen.

Paintings

There is a wealth of paintings produced in the valley. Many are of everyday scenes, but most are of religious significance.

Tangkas are Buddhist paintings. They are sacred scrolls that function as focal points for the practitioner. Traditional Tangkas are painted using natural pigmentations; gold is particularly important. Many depict the stories of the life of Buddha. Most tend to depict a central deity surrounded by lesser figures. Most are from Tibetan Buddhism. Another less common art form is the Tshog-shing, a Tibetan word. In these pictures the central figure is either Gautama Buddha or the long-nosed, yellow-hatted reformer Tsong Khapa. This figure will most often be surrounded by hordes of disciples, witches, divinities, guardians and Yi Dams.

Tangkas were also produced for ordinary people in Tibet at the behest of their religious teachers. These would often depict the sentiments closest to their hearts, such as desires for long life and happiness. The deities would reflect these desires.

Today Tangka painting has developed from being a purely religious skill to become an art form in its own right. Tangkas are now produced for sale to tourists, but retain traditional styles and methods of production. The same artistic skills are used to paint the monastery walls.

Wheel of Life is a graphic representation of life, showing all its mundane aspects. It is a pictorial way of showing us the cycles of life, birth and death into which we are locked by our human desires. These art forms are often found near monastery entrances and follow a general format, with variations depending on the artist.

At the centre are three rather strange animal figures. These are the snake, pig and large bird, which are biting each other. They represent hatred, ignorance and greed. The six main segments depict the realms of different rebirth. The heavenly realm is at the top, and the hellish realm at the bottom. All beings must pass through these different realms. A Buddha figure offers his teachings in each segment. Around the outside are twelve further segments, illustrating the periods of life from birth to death.

The wheel is held by the god Yama, the lord of death, the god who sits in judgement. He is seen tearing and biting it. Buddha is to the right of Yama. He points to a Bodhisattva on the left, who can suggest a way out of the wheel, out of suffering to Nirvana.

Mandalas are other diagrammatic art forms. The geometric shapes within the whole represent the different constituents that help to bring a realisation of enlightenment. Part is the cosmic aspect and other parts are the essence that makes the whole. Circles are the main feature, representing the infinite. Squares represent the form of the universe.

Many of the temples display painted art forms and relate to the deities and gods. We observe that even Buddhism has adopted some erotic art forms of its own. We see in the paintings of Tibetan Buddhism the yab-yum art forms, where gods and demons are in the embrace of female partners. The Yi Dams, who are the tutelary divinities, are invariably shown in yab-yum positions. This emphasises the connection between all religious ideas and the cycles of life in creation, birth and death. So we find the lingam and the yoni depicted in Buddhist art as well. The lingam is depicted in Buddhist art as a lotus flower and the yoni as a turbulent zone. Hence the Buddhist mantra, "Om Mani Padme Hum" (Hail to the Jewel in the Lotus), the idea of life springing forth in an unfolding manner.

Nandi the bull, the vehicle of Shiva

Erotic Art on Temples

It is the more obvious erotic art on the temples that is more difficult to define. When was this first produced, and why?

Many of the pagoda-style temples of the three cities of the valley were built in the Malla period. Although the construction of these temples and pagodas can be defined within a historical period, the art forms that adorn them are not necessarily linked to those dates. Many religious and philosophical influences from earlier periods will have been transformed into art forms and used to decorate the temples. So the actual dating of the temples does not necessarily give clues as to the date and origin of the actual carvings.

We do know that erotic art forms flourished in India a considerable time before they appeared in Nepal. This may not be such a revelation, bearing in mind the natural barriers that we have already mentioned. The style of the art in Nepal though is much less refined than that in India. One has only to see the amazing detail on the famous temples at Khajuraho to see the immediate impact of such art. It is very likely that the appearance of such art forms on the temples cannot be explained by any one single theory.

Why are there Erotic Carvings on the Temples?

Throughout the Kathmandu Valley are an extraordinary number of temples, shrines and sacred places. Amongst them, a large number of these temples are dedicated to the creation of life. More commonly these are referred to as the erotic carvings of Nepal. They exhibit, by graphic depictions and often-surprising carvings, themes almost solely connected with procreation. There is the simple art of stone and the art carved in wood. There is also the rather rare erotic art of paintings and tangkas.

Why should this be so?

Over the centuries, scholars and philosophers have sought explanations to these unusual art forms. Why might they be displayed at sacred places and on temples of holy dispensation? It is obvious at first sight that these carvings are crude and liable to shock. It is conceivable that they are indeed just what they seem. Carvings that will shock the observer and make him feel uncomfortable. Some of these carvings can easily be missed. Many are often found high up and far from the ground. We might then assume that perhaps some are not just for human consumption, but for the gods. Many of these carvings appear on the wooden struts of the pagoda-style temples that characterise the Durbar Squares of the valley's three main cities, Kathmandu, Bhaktapur and Patan. They are often on temples that are sacred to both Hindus and Buddhists. Perhaps it is only the all-seeing eyes and the gods that need to see them.

Outside the Kathmandu Valley there are few erotic carvings. Only in Gorkha and Pokhara are there any well-known images. In Gorkha, there is an unusual carving in the guesthouse of the Royal Gorkha Durbar. It depicts a maiden in a very erotic pose, using a twig from a tree to arouse herself. In Pokhara, on the Bhimsen temple built by the Newari people from Kathmandu, one may also find simple depictions.

Below we list some of the possible theories for the existence of erotic art on temples. For further details, see our book **Erotic Art of the Kathmandu Valley**, also published by Pilgrims.

The Virgin Goddess The Kumari is considered the manifestation of a female deity. In Nepal she can appear as lightning. The erotic carvings might have been placed on the temples to ward off evil spirits and temptations. The temple could be protected from natural elements such as lightning.

Promoting Procreation Were these erotic carvings placed on the temples to encourage procreation in times of falling population? Infant mortality was also very high and parents needed to consider their own future security by having enough offspring to support them in their old age. The carvings could be a focus for these ideas and, with them life would be preserved.

Fertility Another possibility is that the temple art forms represent a positive message of fertility against all the destructive forces in the world; those forces that seek to destroy life. By showing the physical and other life in many forms, the destructive gods are being told to keep their distance. The fact that some carvings illustrate sexual acts between animals and humans is harder to comprehend.

Against Temptation Do these carvings remind those sages and holy men to be on their guard, to warn of difficult paths ahead?

Fear of the Gods As we have already briefly touched upon, fear is another possibility. Whether it is the fear of humans of the gods, or the gods that fear to enter the temple, fear can be a serious contender as an answer. The fear of the Third Eye has its roots once again in Tantra. According to Tantra, when the Third Eye opens one can see to infinity, through the mists of time and across the universe. This could be a frightening idea in itself, enough to want to keep its influence at some distance.

Fear of Evil Do these erotic images keep away the forces of the supernatural, the demons and evil spirits that can manifest as natural destructive phenomenon? But why do they need to be erotic?

Influence of the Kama Sutra Did the descriptive writings of the Kama Sutra translate into art forms that found their way north to Kathmandu? The act of union, Maithuna, has come to represent a basic religious doctrine in Hinduism and in certain aspects of Buddhism. The union of man and woman is considered as the symbol of divine creation, a transformation from duality to union. It simply cannot be that these builders were morally degenerate or pampering to the taste of a decadent public. The sculptors endeavoured to convey the mystic union, the idea of serenity rather than enjoyment. It can be seen how closely the acts convey the meaning of the sutras.

Tantra Perhaps these artistic depictions are more associated with Tantra in its more magical forms. The Tantra associated with the physical means to reach this state is depicted in many art forms, common to both Hindu and Buddhism, involving the sexual embrace. In Buddhist art the embraces are much less provocative.

Kundalini is the flame of creation. It rises like the serpent or snake that coils from within the sexual zones. Kundalini is an abstract notion with great powers. The snake is depicted on many temples. To arouse Kundalini, the life forces and energies must rise through the chakras, the portals of understanding in the subtle body. When Kundalini is activated, the flow of energy can be used to open the mind, to see the true self, enlightenment as to who we really are.

Shiva and Shakti Dominating much of the Hindu religion is the idea of the creation of the universe. In the Shiva-Shakti idea, the central theme is that it is the sexual embrace of the male and female, the embrace of the divine couple, which led to the creation of the universe. Shiva is again the male form. The Shakti is the female as the powering force. Shakti is a Hindu concept, but such female powers are also found in Tantric Buddhism. If the sexual embrace of the divine couple is linked to the creation of the universe, then it would seem likely that depictions of this act on temples would seem quite desirable and logical. We always return to the manifestation of that creation and its worship.

Most of these theories are based on the fact that the act of creation, both from the human perspective and from that of all living things, is the most potent force against destruction; against the end of life as it is known within the finite universe. Without creation there can be no further life. Because this form of Shiva worship is so dominant within the Kathmandu valley and Nepal, its application on the temples as a way of appeasing the destructive forces would seem to be reason enough for such displays.

Kathmandu Durbar Square

ILLUSTRATIONS

1. Kathmandu Durbar Square

3. Market Porter Kathmandu, 1982

2. King Birendra Coronation procession, 1975

4. Dhyani Buddhas, Kathmandu Bahal

5. Sleeping Vishnu Budhanilkantha

6. Boudhnath Stupa

7. Monks at Boudnath

8. Dhum Varahi idol

9. Bhaktapur Durbar Square

10. Street in Bhaktapur

11. Nyatopola Temple, Bhaktapur

12. Changu Narayan, temple door and torana

13. Patan Durbar Square

14. Street scene, Patan

15. Mandala in Bungamati square

16. Chariot wheels – Rato Machhendranath festival

CHAPTER SEVEN
Exploring the Valley: Kathmandu

We can soon begin our trip around the sights of the valley. We begin in Kathmandu and then explore the valley, starting in the north and working around to the west. The cities of Patan, Bhaktapur and Kirtipur will be found within this layout, as well as the three other main sites, Pashupatinath, Boudhanath and Swayambhunath. The order of places described does not constitute any order of preference or interest. Each has its own merits.

The Road to Kathmandu, August 1974.

With the monsoon clouds gathering, we began what turned out to be the last big hill. All around luxuriant vegetation clung to the lush hillsides. A farmer whacked his cow, the obstinate beast being quite contrary and in no mood for ploughing. The terrace was one of thousands that sort of grew up the hillside. The Land Rover crunched down to a lower gear; the road was torturous and unforgiving. But we did have the road all to ourselves; only the noise of our engine and a puzzled dog broke the silence as we climbed upwards.

On the crest of the hill we entered a land of rice fields and toy houses. To our right foothills towered above, also dotted with farmhouses. The houses in the valley were tiny with two floors and overhanging roofs. On a verandah a bamboo baby cot was swinging. Corncobs were drying in the sun and pumpkins clung on to the rooftops. Reaching a large village, Thankot, we stopped at a checkpost to write in a tatty book where we had come from and where we were going. In the distance we could see the monkey temple and the city bathed in the sunlight, shortly to be obliterated by the pending rains. Unfortunately no mountains were showing to the north.

Suddenly the road became a muddy track, no more. We drove on, barely going ten miles an hour. The last part of our journey from England proved the slowest of the entire trip. After crossing an old bridge over a river (the Vishnumati), we stopped at the Hotel Withes, where overlanders could park. We were on the edge of town, with fields of rice down across the road and some small houses nearby, hiding a temple close to another river (the Bagmati at Teku).

North of the hotel was a maze of muddy lanes and the alleys of the old city. Every manner of domestic animal nosed about the rotting food; dung heaps issued forth an indescribable stench. Men scurried about, carrying great loads slung under each end of a bamboo pole. Others struggled under heavy loads in bamboo baskets supported by head straps. Children barely able to walk greeted us with cries of "Namaste".

On the way to Durbar Square, we passed some incredible temples. There was rubbish everywhere; the temples here seemed to defy gravity, a mass of grass was growing on their tiered roofs. Many were in a bad way. Fruit and vegetable sellers seemed to take over the lower plinths of the temples. We found a café wreaking of hash, but just sat down anyway in amazement at this mediaeval scene before us.

Kathmandu, we had arrived.

Kathmandu

We start our journey of discovery in the heart of Kathmandu, at Durbar Square, now protected and designated by UNESCO as a world heritage site.

Durbar Square

The earliest structures we see today in the Durbar Square date from the time of Ratna Malla (1500 AD). Between 1560-74 AD, Mahendra Malla built much of the palace which we see now. He also built the imposing Taleju temple, as well as the Shiva temple and the Jagannath temple in the square.

Approaching from New Road, we come first to the imposing **Hanuman Dhoka** complex on the right. The first temple on the right is the **Lalitpur tower**. The **Basantapur Durbar** is the tall nine-storied structure built around 1770. It is the building in which the coronation of the Shah Kings of Nepal takes place. The Shah Kings originated from Gorkha in central Nepal, from a hilltop palace that still exists today. They united Nepal in the period 1768. Today much of Hanuman Dhoka is a museum, with some vivid and beautiful carvings quite high up on the south side. One can enter on certain days of the week and visit the museum, climbing up within the Basantapur Durbar for a fine view. The museum has objects, photographs and other memorabilia from the Tribhuvan period.

The old hippy hangout and original tourist haunt, **Jochhen Tole**, commonly referred to as **Freak Street**, is to the left here. A couple of guesthouses and cafés still operate. The Monumental Guesthouse and the Century Lodge were two of the first hotels to be opened here. In the 1960s and 70s, most of the hippies and travellers stayed here, with a selection of cafés and restaurants to be found on the street. "Eat at Joe's" was one popular place; buffalo steak and chips was 6 rupees (half a dollar in 1974). "Don't pass me by" and the "New Third Eye" were others, as well as "Aunt Jane's" with its famous chocolate cake.

The Swiss restaurant was another, but apart from greasy rösti, it had the same menu. After the coronation of King Birendra, Freak Street began to decline in favour of Thamel. The hippies left for Pokhara and then Goa.

Sketch Map of Kathmandu Durbar Square

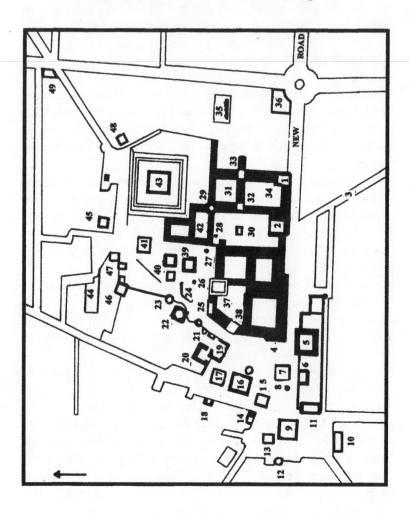

Key to Sketch Map of Kathmandu Durbar Square

1	Lalitpur tower	26	King Pratap Malla column
2	Basantapur tower	27	Hanuman Statue
3	Jochhen Tole	28	Narasingha Statue
4	Gaddi Durbar	29	Panch Mukti Hanuman temple
5	Kumari Bahal House	30	Nasal Chowk
6	Sikhamu Bahal	31	Mul Chowk
7	Trailoyka Narayan temple	32	Kirtipur tower
8	Garuda Statue	33	Bhaktapur tower
9	Kasthamandap	34	Lohan Chowk
10	Simha Sattal	35	Bandarkal sleeping Vishnu
11	Dansa	36	Hotel Classic
12	Gas Kuti Mahadev temple	37	Degutaleju Temple
13	Biseshwori Mahadev	38	Bhagawati temple
14	Ashok Vinayak	39	Jagannath temple
15	Lakshmi Narayan temple	40	Indrapur and Vishnu temples
16	Maju Dewal temple	41	Kakeshwor temple
17	Narayan temple	42	Mohan Chowk
18	Agam Chen Bahal	43	Taleju Temple
19	Shiva Parvati temple	44	Kot square
20	Laykhu Bahal	45	Mahendreshwor temple
21	Taleju Bell	46	Kotelingeshvara temple
22	Chayasin temple	47	Vishnu temple
23	Big Drums	48	Tarani Dev shrine
24	Kala Bhairab	49	Akash Bhairab temple
25	Seto Bhairab		

Kathmandu, February 1975 — A look back at the diary

Took another train to Patna. What a dump. Flew to Kathmandu in a Fokker. Had a great view of the Himalayas coming into the airport; we could easily see Everest, Gauri Shankar and Langtang. The air was so clear, no monsoon clouds this time. The valley was draped in the colours of spring. The Land Rover was completely untouched, safe and sound. It was great to be back, like a second homecoming. We talked a lot to the hotel manager. Even managed to get trek permits and flights sorted for Lukla - $35. Had lunch in Freak Street at Joe's and ate all afternoon in different pie shops. Tried Aunt Jane's chocolate cake - wow! Moved on to the Yellow Star and then the Tibetan Dragon.

We seem to be eating constantly these days. Found some great lemon meringue pies at the 'Chai and Pie' this time. The steak and mashed potatoes at the Yin Yang was great, a bit expensive though at 12 rupees - a dollar. Got some great photos from Swayambhu this time, clear skies with mountains on the northern rim of the valley. It's quite a nice walk out from the city, quite a long way, across the river and through leafy country lanes.

Hugh had four pieces of lemon pie yesterday at the Chai and Pie; perhaps that's why it's called Pig Alley!

Beyond Freak Street to the south are a few old temples, **Om Bahal**, where the Democracy Martyrs often gathered, and a very large open square with more temples. **Lagan Tole** is down here with a few temples, including one for the white Seto Machhendranath, and also the tree which the idol circles as part of its annual festivities.

Continuing along the road, we pass part of the old palace and then come to the large white palace, the **Gaddi Durbar**, built in 1908 by Chandra

Shumshere Rana after his visit to England. On the left, across the street is the Kumari's house (**Kumari Bahal**), which is guarded by two stone lions. This building was constructed by Jaya Prakash Malla in the mid-18th century. The Kumari infant is found from among the Newari Sakya clan, who are Buddhists, but she is revered as a Hindu Goddess. There are various tantric rites invoked in order to select this child goddess, who will normally be no more than four years old when she is chosen. She lives in this house until she has spilt blood, either through puberty or injury. During the festival of Indra Jatra she is taken out into the streets, dressed in fine silks and gold.

Next to the Kumari Bahal is the **Sikhamu Bahal**. In its untidy courtyard are some Buddhist chaityas. Buddhist texts were produced here and the priest is responsible for choosing the Kumari goddess. The priest is known as the Raj Guru and is the head of the Nepali Buddhist community.

In the main square we come to the **Trailokya Narayan Mandir**, which is a Vishnu temple built in 1690 under the Queen Mother, Riddhi Lakshmi. It was damaged by the earthquake of 1934, but restored using the original parts. There is a black Garuda idol on the south side of the temple. During the festival of Indra Jatra, men dress up as the ten incarnations of Vishnu and gather here.

Heading off to the southwest, we come to the **Maru Tole** area, in which stands the massive **Kasthamandap** temple. Its name means house of wood, and it is said to have been built from the wood of a single tree. Kathmandu gets its name from this temple. The structure is unusual in that its lower precinct is open and once provided a resting-place for holy men. Yogi **Gorakhnath** was one such preacher. Images of Ganesh adorn the four cardinal directions inside the temple. The central image with a trident behind it, sitting like the Buddha, is Gorakhnath. Some locals call it Gola Maya.

The **Simha Sattal** to the south of the tole contains an image of Garuda and a shrine to Hari Krishna. On the north side is a large three-tiered complex called the **Dansa** or **Kabindrapur**. This building dates from Pratap Malla in 1673 and is now part shrine and part Guthi house. It is dedicated to Vishnu as Narasingha, half man, and half lion.

The small shrine of **Ashok Vinayak** (or Binayak) beside the Kasthamandap is found adjacent to a gilded image of Ganesh's vehicle, the rat. The Ashok Vinayak is dedicated to the elephant god Ganesh, who is one of the most popular gods in the valley. The gilded image of the god is beautifully set within the shrine. This is very important to the people of

Kathmandu and is worshipped continually most days. It is sometimes referred to as the Ganesh Maru. There is also a small bell here. An image of Hanuman stands in the Lakshmi Narayan temple by the bell.

Just behind the temple to the west side, near Ganesh, is a narrow lane that leads down towards the river. This lane was known as **Pig Alley** until the early eighties. Down here were a great selection of pies, tarts and cakes for the tourists and hippies of that time. Such names as "Chai and Pie", "Pancha's Pies" and "The Upper Crust Pie Shop" were all firm favourites. The hash cakes and hash brownies were also pretty popular! The cafés here were all old, traditional Newari-style houses with low doorways and low ceilings. Outside in the filthy lane, pigs lived, browsing and chewing amongst the organic waste. There is a sunken bath down here and further down by the river is the Kankeshwari goddess temple. See details below.

Retrace your steps back into the square, towards the white neo-classical Rana building. In the main part of the square, near the white Indian-looking temple, is the tall pagoda-style temple of Mahadev, also called the **Shivamandir** or **Maju Dewal** temple. Erotic carvings can be seen on the struts on three sides of the temple. This temple was once the haunt of the freaks and hippies, whose notorious presence inadvertently gave Kathmandu such an aurora of mysticism in the late sixties and early seventies. Where are they now?

A little to the north is another imposing temple dedicated to Vishnu as Narayan. Fruit and vegetable sellers are often found here. On the west side is another temple, the **Agam Chen**; the bahal behind it is rather modernised now. The shop next to it has been tastefully renovated though. The elaborate wooden temple with five doors ahead on the left is dedicated to **Shiva**, this time with his benign wife **Parvati** on display. Both are seen in mortal form, observing the scenes below. They are also perhaps looking for the long-departed hippies. Bahadur Shah Rana built this temple.

Across the street is a picturesque smallish temple growing out of the shops next to the Rana palace. It is devoted to **Bhagawati**. Behind the Shiva Parvati temple is a **gigantic bell** dedicated to Taleju, made in 1797. The bell is only rung at times of offering to goddess Degutaleju. Behind the bell is the **Laykhu Bahal** with some amazing woodcarving on a torana above the main shrine. The main deity here is sometimes on view before nine in the mornings.

After a couple of small temples devoted to Vishnu and Saraswati, we come to the **Chayasin** temple. This octagonal structure is dedicated to

Krishna playing his flute. Built in 1649, it was built in memory of Pratap Malla's dead queens. The deities Rukmini and Satyabhama are also enshrined here. Two gigantic drums are found high above the street here. Animal sacrifices must be performed before either is struck.

Nearby to the drums on the opposite side of the street is the giant grotesque figure of the black **Kala Bhairab**—the God of wrath and terror, another manifestation of Shiva. To this day no one knows where this massive stone image of the god came from. It is believed to have been found, face down, in a field during the Malla Kings' period.

From here we need to retreat a little, and stop at the corner, with the entrance to **Hanuman Dhoka** itself ahead east. Sitting here, hiding behind a latticed screen, is the hideous **Seto (white) Bhairab**, who is only revealed and worshipped during Indra Jatra. The massive image is actually a golden colour and quite monstrous. Also here at the corner is a column dedicated to King Pratap Malla, patron of much of the square. His prayer room, the **Degutaleju** or **Degutale Mandir**, is seen from here. The Degutaleju temple is dedicated to the tantric goddess and is accessible only from the palace. Its tiers have been constructed on top of an existing building.

Hanuman Dhoka

Continue ahead now to the Hanuman Dhoka itself. Beside the entrance gate, the statue of the monkey god Hanuman stands guard. He appears as a rounded, reddened stone shape sheltering under an umbrella. The image is said to keep evil plagues, diseases, demons and devils away from the palace. Two stone lions with images of Shiva and Parvati seated on them guard the golden gateway to the palace.

Before the earthquake of 1934 the palace was much more extensive. It was a creation of the Malla Kings and was used by them. Inside the palace we come to **Nasal Chowk** where the Shah Kings are crowned, although few ever resided here. On the left is an image of **Narasingha**, the lion man who is killing a demon. He is an incarnate of Vishnu and is a protector who cannot be killed by demons. Also in this courtyard we find the five-tiered round temple called **Panch Mukhi Hanuman**.

The **Mul Chowk** on the east side is not accessible to non-Hindus, being a private area for the kings and the preserve of the goddess Taleju. Ritual animal sacrifices take place here during Dashain, when Hindus can enter. The **Lohan Chowk** was the living area of the Malla Kings and has four towers, one at each corner. The **Basantapur Durbar** is one; the others are the **Kirtipur** tower, a copper-roofed structure, the **Bhaktapur** and **Lalitpur** (Patan) towers. Each was built by money from the vassal city-states after unification under Prithvi Narayan Shah. The **Vilas Mandir**, the 'building of luxury', is also here between the Basantapur and Lalitpur towers. It offers views over the Chowk.

Further in are the gardens of **Bandarkal**, where another **sleeping Vishnu** is located. This is not accessible to the public. In fact this sleeping Vishnu sits in a very large pool or tank, and can just be seen through the branches of a tree from the very top of the Hotel Classic, (formerly Hotel Crystal). Tea can be taken up here as well, but the view of the Vishnu is a couple of stories up from the tea garden.

Much of the palace was restored in the mid-seventies around the time of King Birendra's coronation. Local skilled artisans, carpenters and builders undertook the work. The British architect, John Sanday, who subsequently worked on restoration at Angkor Wat in Cambodia, was a key co-ordinator in this UNESCO project.

Durbar Square North End

On exiting the palace, we come back to the statue of the monkey god **Hanuman**. The **Jagannath** temple is between the monkey god statue and the black **Bhairab**. Here we find more erotic displays. At one time it could be recognised by the painted eyes and trident on each door. These are the signs of Shiva, but they have faded in recent years. Look up at the struts here on all sides to find the amazing variety of carvings.

A cluster of small temples and shrines are found next to the Jagannath temple. The **Vishnu/Narayan** and **Indrapur** temples are the bigger two; both have some carved struts higher up. The next temple is devoted to **Kakeshwor**. Behind these across the street are more shrines, devoted to **Shiva**, **Kotelingeshvara**, **Nil Varahi** and **Mahavishnu**, about which little is recorded.

From here, your eyes will be directed upwards to the imposing **Taleju** temple, the tallest temple in Kathmandu. Taleju is another destructive form of Kali. The temple gates are rarely opened. The temple stands some 40 metres high and was built by King Mahendra Malla in 1564. The whole temple stands on a raised plinth with twelve levels. Small shrines surround the temple. A fine gajura tops this tall edifice. It was here that the last of the Malla kings sought refuge before the invading Gurkhas.

On the first full moon of January, the spirit of Vishnu as Narayan is carried in a kalash, an urn filled with holy water. It is brought from the Changu Narayan temple, north of Bhaktapur, to Asan and Indra Chowk, and then to the Taleju temple, where the living goddess Kumari blesses the King. The King is considered a reincarnate of Vishnu, as Narayan. The priests are the only others allowed access, except during Dashain when the blood sacrifices occur. At one time human sacrifice took place. Taleju is a bloodthirsty incarnation of goddess Durga.

At the far end of the square is the courtyard known as the **Kot Square**. This is where Jung Bahadur Kunwar Rana seized power after the Kot Massacre in 1846. The marble temple at the far north end is the **Mahendraswor** temple, which actually dates back to 1561 and was built during Mahendra Malla's reign. This is a Shiva temple and contains a lingam. Nandi guards the temple. The temple has been modernised considerably. Just along from here is a narrow alley behind the Taleju temple that leads to the **Tarani Dev** shrine.

Hippy, Old Kathmandu

Sketch Map of Old Kathmandu

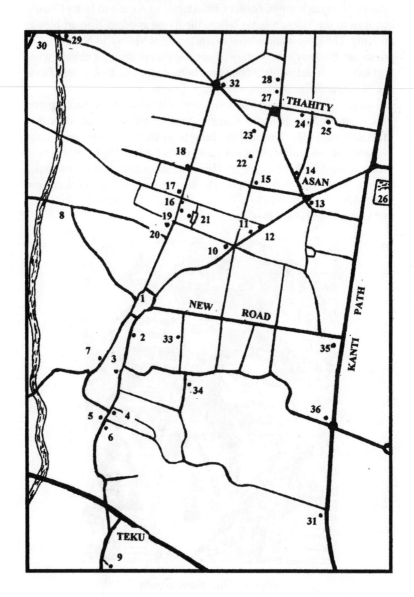

Key to Sketch Map of Old Kathmandu

1	Durbar Square	19	Pulucka Dega Shiva temple
2	Atko Narayan temple	20	Yetakha Bahal stupa
3	Harishanker temple	21	Itum Bahal
4	Jaisi Dewal	22	Kathesimbhu Stupa
5	Ramchandra Mandir	23	Naghal Bahal
6	Tukan Bahan Stupa	24	Musya Bahal
7	Bhimsen temple	25	Chusya Bahal
8	Kankeshwari temple	26	Rani Pokhari lake
9	Pachali Bhairab	27	Bhagawati temple
10	Akash Bhairab	28	Kwa Bahal
11	Jana Bahal Seto	29	Indryani temple
	Machhendranath	30	Bijeshwori
12	Kali Chamunda	31	Jagannath temple
13	Annapurna temple	32	Chhetrapati
14	Jwala Mai	33	Freak Street
15	Bangemunda	34	Om Bahal
16	Deshe Maru Jhya window	35	Royal Nepal Airlines
17	Sweta Kali / Naradevi temple	36	G.P.O.
18	Raktakali temple		

South from Durbar Square

From Kathmandu Durbar Square take the left of the two streets, Chikan Mugal Street, towards the south from the Kasthamandap temple. Along the way are a couple of interesting temples and shrines. First you come to a Vishnu temple, **Atko Narayan**, which has three tiers. The lower level has no erotic carvings, but the second level has some simple ones. Almost out of sight, on the third level up, are some basic couples interlocked. This temple is unusual, in that it has erotic art but is not a Shiva temple.

As you make your way along this old street, on the right is a small temple with erotic art; this is the **Harishanker** temple. Further down you come to another three-tiered temple with very steep access steps. This is the **Jaisi Dewal** Shiva temple, built around 1688. It has erotic art on the lower tiers. Across the road, in a lower building, is a small door into a courtyard. This is the **Ramchandra** (Mandir) temple with Hanuman, shaded by a parasol, guarding the entrance. Krishna is seen on the central torana above the central shrine, with cows and gopis. Some erotic art is on view and there is a small marble shrine with lingam plus an old inscription plate. Some holy cows are kept in the rooms inside!

Across the street is a gilded mini-Swayambhu called **Tukan**, which is over thirty feet high. It is six hundred years old. The Dhyani Buddhas are found around the base of the main dome plus four Taras and other images.

The **Bhimsen Mandir** is further south on the next street over to the south. It is a three-tiered temple with a lattice-panelled first floor. It is rectangular in shape, gaily painted and rather gaudy. The main idol is up the steps on the first floor. Bhimsen, the god of merchants, appears here as a red larger-than-life-size idol. No entry is permitted for non-Hindus, sadly, as it's an impressive room.

The **Kankeshwari** temple is another startling sight located down Maru Tole (Pig Alley) just past a large stupa by the river and close to the suspension bridge. This three-tiered temple has gilded roofs. Buffalo horns adorn the east side. Lions and dragon-like guardians are the protectors. There are some erotic figures, one with animals performing. The Goddess has eight arms and is very skeletal in appearance on the main wooden torana and elsewhere. Her stomach is rather hollow; she must have dysentery. Large gilded banners are found on the north side. Other images are shown on toranas, with crowns or garlands of skulls standing on bodies or corpses.

The main ground floor deity is small and set in an open spacious area under the structure. The ceiling above the deity inside is gilded, decorated and circular. Bells are everywhere. The site of the Kankeshwari temple dates from around the 7th - 8th century. Before the early 1800s, stone throwing and ritual human sacrifices to the goddess Kali, as Kankeshwari, took place here. It was abolished at that time.

The goddess is also depicted in a small shrine with an amazingly large pipal tree growing over and through it. Even the top gajura is still intact amongst the roots. Ganesh here is about to fall backwards into the river. When we visited, a wedding party had gathered to pay homage to the goddess. The band members, in their bright red jackets, were playing their musical instruments with vigour just up the street.

Continuing South

From Ramchandra Mandir follow the lane until you come out at Teku, on the main road to the Kalimati suburbs, Naubise and Pokhara.

A road opposite leads on down to the river Bagmati. Heading left, you will come to **Pachali Bhairab**. This consists of a very large pipal tree, a reclining corpse (not Vishnu) for blood rituals and a small shrine. Pachali Bhairab is the shrine of the five lingams, which are hidden in the small recess of the floor. Images here are of Ganesh, Kumar, Ajima and Varahi. When we visited two filthy hyperactive rats jumped out and started to brawl madly, totally oblivious of the worshippers or the serenity of the scene. At this shrine, Shiva appears in a form of terror and destruction as Bhairab. The two rats may not live long; Bhairab's anger was surely aroused.

There are different legends told about this shrine. Some say, as its name suggests, that five lingams are buried in the shrine. A more colourful story relates the tale of a girl who looked after some pigs. This virgin girl fell in love with a handsome young man. When she became pregnant by him, she asked him who he was. He initially refused to say, for he was none other than Bhairab. After much time the young man eventually relented, sadly revealing his truly hideous demon face. She fled in horror, abandoning her baby in the road. Bhairab fled back into his hole and all that can be seen of him at Pachali is his buttock! The baby grew up to be Shiva's son Ganesh.

If you now head further south towards the Bagmati River, you pass some decrepit buildings surrounding a Shiva temple. From the riverside, go through an elaborate wooden doorway into this courtyard. Here is the **Laxmeshwar Mahadev** temple. This temple has some rather unconventional but excellent artwork. One strut graphically shows a baby being pulled at birth. Another shows a dog doing naughty things. The temples around here and along the riverbank towards the Patan Bridge, to the east, are in a very sorry state of decay and disrepair. As long ago as 1993 restoration was about to be undertaken, but alas little work has been done yet.

Just by the old suspension bridge is the main cremation ghat at Teku. Just west of here is the confluence of the Vishnumati and Bagmati rivers. Here at this sacred spot these two rivers are said to be linked to the mythical **Saraswati** river and the Ganges and Jamuna rivers. The location of the Allahabad Khumbh Mela is also said to be where the two real rivers join the mythical Saraswati.

Heading east towards the Patan bridge, you pass numerous tumbledown shrines, ghats and temples, many inhabited by squatters and poor people. The **Tripureshwar Mahadev** temple is next. This large temple is a little shabby and was built in 1818 by a wife of the assassinated Rana, Bahadur Shah. A trident here indicates it is a Shiva temple; there is a gilded image of the queen who built it sitting on a snake stone pillar, as well as Nandi the bull, Shiva's vehicle. Just by the Patan bridge is the **Kalmochan** temple, a strange mix of Hindu and Moghul style, with massive gilded serpents clearly visible. The ashes of the murdered noblemen from the Kot Massacre are said to have been hidden here.

North and East from Durbar Square

If you continue northeast from the Kot Square, you come to **Indra Chowk**. Here is the **Akash Bhairab** temple that was completely remodelled during 2001-2002. This version of Bhairab is the sky Bhairab, usually blue in colour. Non-Hindus cannot enter. Four gilded dragons guard the first floor shrines. A Shiva temple sits here, but it is often covered with rug and shawl sellers and their wares.

Continuing further northeast, the temple shrine of the **Seto** (white) **Machhendranath** is found, deep in the markets of old Kathmandu. It is in the **Jan Bahal**/Jana Bahal or, more correctly, Jamal Bahal. This shrine is revered by Kathmandu Newari Buddhists and is a vision of metal, gilded artwork, chaityas, and a fair few pigeons.

Even before you enter, a wealth of imagery decorates the entrance from the busy street of sellers and shopkeepers. On the right is a column with the Dhyani Buddhas facing east and west, the Akshobhya and Amitabha Buddhas. Above the main entrance is a golden torana with a central east-facing Buddha with figures each side representing dharma and sangha. Sometimes musicians will be playing haunting melodies as you go into the main bahal. Once inside, on the right is a small wood-latticed chamber containing a dark, stern-looking Buddha. The strange golden statue that sits close to the entrance is a European-looking lady (said possibly to be Queen Victoria) used for burning incense. Sitting high on columns are four figures facing the central temple. These are Manjushri, a Tara, Prajnaparmita and a Lokeshvara. Closer to the main shrine are two Green Taras on top of two more columns, with a large abstract stone between them, the Kanak Chaitya. There are also many chaityas with different Bodhisattvas and Buddhas.

The central temple is cloaked in metal and gilded ornamentation, with two tiers of amazing iconography. The central deity is the white idol of Seto Machhendranath looking as serene as the Buddha. The small white idol itself is covered in jewels, fine robes and an abundance of colourful flowers. It is attended constantly by worshippers. Butter lamps adorn the entrance area. The Buddhist deity Machhendranath is also a vision of Avalokiteshvara when white, and a version of Padmapani Lokeshvara when red.

On the entrance toranas above the idol is a magnificent image of the eleven-headed version of Avalokiteshvara, flanked by Tara on the left torana and Manjushri on the right torana. On the left (west) side of the temple within the metal trellising is a door with some superb golden Mahakala images reminiscent of Bhairab. Above are the one hundred and eight painted visions of Lokeshvara set behind glass, and above these are more wooden carved images of the various Lokeshvaras on the temple struts. On the east side, the entire façade is decorated by thirty-six em-bossed, gilded images of the different Bodhisattvas, as well as other mag-nificent imagery. The door here has eight figures showing the Newari Siddhis, those Tantrics who have attained perfection and have superhu-man powers.

According to legends and folk tales, clay diggers found the idol of Machhendranath. They were excavating an old well in Jamal near Rani Pokhari during the reign of Yaksha Malla, mid 15th century.

You can exit the Jan Bahal west to **Kel Tole**, famous for its pottery. Elephant flowerpots from Thimi and many other clay products can be bought here.

Continuing northeast, you come shortly to the **Kali Chamunda** temple. This small temple has eyes on the front as well as three images in brass above the door. Some erotic art in wood can be seen here. Continuing again northeast, we come to the crowded and frantic area of **Asan Tole**. The vegetable and fruit markets are now a short distance to the northwest.

The **Annapurna** temple stands on the south side, a temple with a brass roof and a glittering array of decorations; this temple is in honour of the goddess who gives bountiful harvest. Annapurna is a manifestation of Lakshmi, goddess of prosperity and wealth. Two gilded beasts guard the temple and there are also two odd characters, a skeleton and a fat man in shorts! A pataka, a metal strip, flows down the temple to help the gods to come to earth. Some brass snakes ring the base area.

The two smaller shrines here are devoted to Ganesh and Vishnu. Northwest of Asan Tole is a temple called **Jwala Mai**, a mother goddess temple with some erotic carvings very high up on the top tier of the pagoda.

The **Bangemunda** Temple is also called **Ikha Narayan**. There are some graceful figures on the struts, two on each side. Those on the west-facing side have extra small figures resting on the main figure's waist, with hands almost touching the voluminous breasts of the goddesses, who are nude above the waist. Each deity is sitting on an anguished-faced figure. At first glance one would associate this shrine with the mother goddesses, but Shiva is not in evidence here.

West of Indra Chowk are a number of temples, shrines and bahals in the area of Naradevi. Here is an elaborate window called **Deshe Maru Jhya**.

Nearby, going north to the Naradevi area, is the **Netamaru Ajima**, a three-tiered temple with gilded roofs and delightful carvings. This temple is sometimes known as **Akachen** on maps. Locals often call it **Sweta Ajima** or **Sweta Kali** (White Kali). Some refer to it as the **Naradevi** temple. It is a temple of the Astha Matrikas, mother goddesses, with struts depicting them. Although only two carvings show coupling of the figures, the other figures are almost more erotic for their close intimacy. The main deity is skeletal, similar to that seen at Kankeshwari, with a seriously empty stomach. The deity sits on five skulls. There are two toranas above the entrance with a red Chhepu above. This is the temple of five skulls and is richly decorated on the first floor at the roof edges with many skulls to ward off disease and plague.

Just north is an amazingly old and crumbling bahal with intricate windows on all sides; sadly on one side it is on the verge of collapse. We called it **Rabies Bahal** as there is a clinic there, offering rabies vaccinations and treatment in early morning and late afternoon.

Two other temples here about are **Raktakali**, a small, totally gilded one-storey shrine dedicated to Kali. There is no idol as such in the shrine. The **Pulucka Dega** is a Shiva temple along from Sweta Ajima towards Durbar Square and has erotic art. It is three-tiered and has a lingam inside.

There are a couple of large all-seeing stupas in the bahal squares in the area of old Kathmandu. One is in the **Yetakha Bahal**. The stupa has a bulging upper dome and gilded levels. Across the street are some superb windows by the entrance.

Itum Bahal, near Naradevi, is a very large open bahal. This courtyard, according to legends, was home to **Guru Mapa**. Guru Mapa was an ogre who devoured children until pacified by the boy King Keschandra. He is now placated by the sacrifice of a buffalo, which keeps him from returning. This occurs during the end of the Holi festival and is peculiar to this bahal.

On the west side of the main quadrangle are two places of worship. One is a Buddhist shrine with three Tara images. Butter festivities take place here some days. The other shrine is further south on the west side, indicated as a school. This smaller courtyard is being repaired. There is a very unusual standing Buddhas statue with four images combined in chaitya form. A black Buddha sits in the main shrine, with a wooden torana above the entrance. Six struts above each have three-faced deities to admire. Guru Mapa is depicted on a copper plaque on the new façade to the north at the right end. Other scenes are said to depict the temptations posed to the Buddha.

Exiting to the south, you will see a very detailed torana protected by mesh. Go out here and go left down an atmospheric dark alley to return to Indra Chowk.

Kathesimbhu Stupa, which is quite large, was built in the 17th century as an imitation of Swayambhunath, being more easily accessible to the townspeople. It is often referred to as **mini-Swayambhu**. The square has been modernised recently, but its origins probably go back to the Licchavi period. There is a shrine here dedicated to Sitala or Harati, the goddess of smallpox, in the northwest corner. A large chaitya sits in a yoni on northeast side, together with other chaityas. The stupa has the usual five Dhyani

Buddhas around the base of the dome. Very new construction on the north side is now replacing the quaint windowed old buildings with a new monastery and temple.

Naghal Bahal is in a hidden, newly-restored corner with a three-tiered temple and a lower roof over the main door. It is usually closed. The floors are latticed and the torana has a Manjushri-like figure on it.

Look out for the toothache shrine, a cluster of nails and coins/washers, where anyone with toothache goes to worship in order to alleviate their pain. The name of this deity is **Vaisya Dev**.

Continuing almost north, one reaches **Thahiti Square**, where there is a small stupa. Musicians were to be seen here often in the late seventies and early eighties, but no more. Divine musicians in metal are however seen on the Shiva temple here. Just east into Jyatha is the **Musya Bahal**, guarded by two stone lions. Musya Bahal has another elaborate torana with a three-faced four-armed deity. There are thirty animal-faced protectors.

Further on is **Chusya Bahal**. This temple was built in 1649 and has been restored. Two lions guard it. Chusya Bahal has an elaborate wood torana depicting Prajnaparmita, a Buddhist goddess flanked with dancing attendants. Inside is a two-storey temple. The deities here are quoted as being Mahakala, Ganesh, Vajrasattva and Tara, plus the two donors. Potters were seen here until the early nineties, still using their feet to power the wheels. The bahal is newly restored, but often closed.

Kwa Bahal is located north again from Thahiti Square and once had its own Kumari. It is now run down and guarded by unhappy growling dogs! Some fading painted wall depictions are set above the main house. This Kumari here was unusual, being a purely Buddhist Kumari. Also north of Thahiti, just opposite to J. B. Art Buddha shop, is a small Bhagawati temple with a restored entrance.

Look in almost any bahal around here and you will find a shrine or temple in a state of disrepair. In the quest for modernisation, new buildings are replacing much of the old city. Some are pleasing, but others are not so fine. Of course no one wants to live in an old house these days, quite understandably, but it is very sad that the old style has been lost. Here and there are modern structures done very well in the old style. The pressures of modern life in the developing world are of much greater concern at present than preserving the old aesthetic beauty. Maybe in time this will change, as has happened in Europe where old styles are desirable and old buildings are respected and cared for. To see what Kathmandu was like even twenty years ago, we must head for Bhaktapur.

Now we are almost back in Thamel, where the gods of money, materialism and alcohol are worshipped by both tourists and locals!

The Kathmandu Guest House

The Kathmandu Guest House was the creation of Karna Sakya in 1970. For him it was a big departure from the accepted traditions of the Sakya clans to become involved in the fledgling tourist business. The building originally belonged to Kumar Narsingh Rana; the designer of Singha Durbar. It had thirteen rooms and its ballroom was a meeting place where the Rana aristocracy dined and danced.

In 1977 I first stayed at the Kathmandu Guest House. To be precise it was in the courtyard, where I slept in the back of the Exodus truck we had driven from London in a month. It was normal to do such things when you worked for an overland company. The Kathmandu Guest House then comprised of low-ceilinged rooms downstairs, rooms with padlocked doors above and the magnificent stately ballroom above them.

On the left, as you crossed the courtyard, was the Tibetan restaurant and some more old rooms above that. The garden was fine and the crumbling buildings on the south side were empty.

In 1979, at the Tashi Takgay Tibetan restaurant, two Tibetan refugees worked behind the counter. Tukten and Urgen were from Kalimpong and worked all hours of the day and much of the night. They usually slept in the restaurant as well. A Tibetan girl, Tashi, generally managed the place. Her brother and sister-in-law had a carpet factory. Outside a Sikh fortuneteller was to be found reading palms and telling everyone about their "Happy life". Mr Singh was there for ten years or more.

A small boy ran about the courtyard offering help to tourists.

In the Guest House, Sohan Shrestha seemed to have been there forever, efficiently overseeing check-ins. In the Natraj travel office, which opened some years later, was Hari, who could be relied upon to know every flight arrival time and every cancellation.

Just outside the gate, Tsering Dolkar ran a trekking gear shop. Tsering Dolkar's father came from the Khampa region. He was part of the guard unit for the Dalai Lama's Norbu Lingka summer residence, and escaped with some of the Dalai Lama's party in 1959. Her mother was from Lhasa. As some of the original early Tibetan refugees, they first met in India.

Where are they now?

Ganesh

Indeed, where have they gone?

The restaurant changed its name to become the Astha Mangal, meaning the eight auspicious signs of Tibet. Paintings of the Potala and scenes from Tibetan folktales adorned the inside. Later it changed again to become a Newari restaurant called Las Kus, and again to become Bahal Café in late 2003. Tukten sadly lost a child and his wife. Both he and Urgen managed to get to Australia, working for a trekker in his factory. It took them over a year to get Nepali passports by various means. After some years in Australia, they received an immigrant amnesty. Urgen was last heard of as a driver at the Indian Embassy in Sydney.

The Tibetan girl married Chris, an Australian, and worked in a travel company until she owned it. Mr Singh never made a fortune, but smiled until he passed away. Sohan still runs Guest Relations at the Guest House, after running a hotel in Pokhara for some years until the downturn in tourism forced him back to Kathmandu. Hari still ran the Natraj office in early 2003, but travelled to work by motorcycle. Now rumour has it he has gone to the bright lights of the USA.

The small boy became bigger, worked for Himalayan Encounters at the Guest House, went to Australia and married. His younger brother now works for Himalayan Encounters. Tsering progressed to reading the News in English on Nepal Television, when it first started broadcasting. Later she opened a hotel in Lazimpat, and is still involved in the carpet business.

A younger generation of the Sakya family now runs the Guest House, and hundreds of hotels and cafés have opened in Thamel.

Thamel

In the tourist quarter of Kathmandu, in Thamel, are three smaller temples located off **Tri Devi Marg**, not far from the Kaiser Library building (Education Dept.) and the Royal Palace. Here the three temples were probably built around 1768 and dedicated to the goddesses **Dakshinkali**, **Manakamana** and (another) **Jwala Mai**. The Dakshinkali temple is the one furthest from the road. At one time, not so long ago, a large field with many grazing cows was located adjacent to the temples. The main temple for erotic art here is the central temple devoted to Manakamana, but the art is fairly simple. The dogs are rather busy on the temples around here! (See Dakshinkali section also.)

The **Thamel Temple**, also known as **Bhagwan Bahal**, is set in a largish area and has some old legends about traders linked to it (see Festivals). The compound is being engulfed and rather overwhelmed by the surrounding high modern structures these days. A scarlet image of Chakandeo is found here. It is not often open though, and rather sad. A small shrine opposite fell down in the late nineties, and is merely marked by some new concrete shrines.

The whole area of Thamel, which has become the main tourist area of Kathmandu, has changed radically since 1980, when the first modern buildings began to be erected. Previously many traditional residential houses existed here, with a few larger compounds with 1960-era houses. One temple collapsed in the early eighties; the site has not been built on, but nothing remains of the temple. The first restaurants in the area were Utse, Jamaly and K.C.'s, all housed in quaint, somewhat tumbledown houses. The Tibetan-run Astha Mangal at the Kathmandu Guest House had a very atmospheric ambience with Tibetan paintings, and was like a monastery inside. In the late seventies only the Kathmandu Guest House, the Star Hotel, the Asia Hotel and later the Tukche Peak (now Pilgrims Book House) provided rooms for guests. Today the quiet residential aspect of Thamel has long gone under a rush of modernisation and development. But the Thamel temple is worth a visit and, despite all the trappings of tourism, Thamel remains a pleasant haven for guests.

Mister K.C., one of old Kathmandu's most colourful characters.

K.C.'s story started with humble beginnings and limited schooling. But he had a vivid imagination and a strong desire to travel and see the world. From his early days as a waiter in the hotel Soaltee Oberoi, he learned what foreigners wanted - "Would you like sugar, milk, sir?" - and had soon gained the contacts that would help him to get a job working for, of all things, the Royal Nepal Shipping Corporation. Flying from Kathmandu to Calcutta and then on to Karachi with Japan Air Lines, he then sailed via Cape Town to London with a cargo of jute. Sometimes the sea was so rough that the food would sail right off the tray... but that is just the beginning of his long story...

Gradually he got to know foreigners' eating habits and gained much experience in dealing with their appetites. It was his restaurant that really started the growth of European-style food in Thamel. K.C. himself was always there, with his long flowing hair and a cigarette in his mouth. He looked more like a hippie than the real hippies! His was the very first "sizzling steak" and salad. People would see the clouds of steam go sizzling by and say "Mmmm... What's that? I'll try one of those... "His was also the very first cheesecake, made with Kraft cheese. And so began a success story.

K.C.'s first began in Pig Alley near Freak Street; buff steak was then three rupees, fifty paisa at his place called 'Bag End'. He was one of the first to move up to Thamel. His restaurant was first established across the road from its current place, and later moved into a kind of lean-to that was half connected to a Newari house behind it. The whole street had old two and three-storied brick and wooden houses on the north side. Each house had pretty windows but no glass; some were quite ornate.

On the south side was a high wall and a large vegetable garden, which in fact only disappeared below modern developments very recently.

In the early days there was no furniture - people would sit on the floor, as indeed they can still do now, in traditional Nepali style with cushions. But then he moved on to having seating for sixteen, and gradually the restaurant evolved into what it is today; still famous for its sizzling steaks and fabulous cheesecakes. And although he is no longer directly involved in the management, he still provides them with delicious fresh avocados from his out-of-town garden. The cheesecake is still the same mouth-watering delight, an erotic art of deserts.

And so what does K.C. stand for? Is it Kaput Crazy, as he used to say, or King of Cuisine?

During a recent visit to his house for tea, Karna Sakya, the owner of the Kathmandu Guest House, entertained us with some fascinating information about early developments in Thamel. Thamel was mostly open fields in the 1950s, with traditional valley houses belonging to Brahmin and Chettri families. These people lived virtually out-of-town in those days, and were not able to live in the Newari heart of Kathmandu in the Asan and Indra Chowk area—the zone of Buddhist bahals.

After the first democratic movement and the fall of the Ranas, some civil servants with money came in, from distant towns like Tansen, and built modern houses with plaster walls, set in large gardens within Thamel. Two examples are what is currently called the 'North West Corner', formerly the old Rainbow Café, and the Brezel Bakery café. Here the old house is still seen under the new concrete brick façade. This was once the 'Up and Down' bar; the floor did the same when dancing took place late at night until the police closed it down. Most of the bars were closed down in the early eighties, for reasons such as 'rowdiness' and 'a bad influence on young Nepali boys' who joined in this previously unheard-of novelty.

The Joker near the Bistro Restaurant was one of the first casualties. The Bistro was the only place where you could hear the news in the early eighties. It broadcast the Radio Nepal News in English at eight o'clock every evening; the only source of news then apart from the government-censored 'Rising Nepal'.

After the Ranas lost power, many of them could not keep up the maintenance of such opulent buildings. Kumar Narsingh Rana sold part of his palace to the Sakya family. In 1970 Karna Sakya took part of this to open a hotel. An attached old wing was in disrepair and knocked down by a brother of the Rana in the late seventies, so Karna bought the strip and built the new wing of the hotel in 1984. The rest, as they say, is history!

Jamaly and Utse 1979

The Jamaly restaurant was a firm favourite, being close to the Utse, a popular watering hole in Thamel located in a small tole where the narrow road opened out. All about here were two and three-storied Newari brick and timber houses. An ancient three-tiered pitha 'temple' sat on the road leading to the Kathmandu Guest House, leaning dramatically to the north. One day an overland truck nudged its first tier and the angle of lean worsened. Sadly the temple fell down some years later.

The ceiling of the Jamaly restaurant was low, as they all were. The entry was up three tricky little steps and inside the place was decorated with woven bamboo panels. The lights were dim, if they were on at all. All that Narayan cooked was great, but the pies and chocolate cakes were a work of art. Narayan started in Pig Alley too. This was the place to come for desserts of all kinds. The parking was easy too. Only bicycles, rickshaws, cows, dogs and the odd taxi passed by. In Tridevi Marg three overgrown temples sat in a compound surrounded by a large field. The field extended all the way to the old Royal Hotel, the first hotel in Kathmandu and now the Election Commission building. Cows grazed on the field.

> *On the other side of Tridevi Marg was a high wall, and nothing more except the Kaiser Library building that stands today. Hundreds of bats hung from the tall trees adjacent to the new Royal Palace.*
>
> *And Narayan today? His large restaurant is near Chhetrapati, with pies and cakes as always. Utse too has reincarnated itself in Jyatha.*

The guthi system of social responsibility and communal tasks started to break down some years ago. Fewer people in the old days were fully employed, and they had more time to contribute to the system. Nowadays, farmers are no longer able to give half their income to the communal guthi for temple maintenance and other socially accepted duties. The pressures of modern life and lack of time have hastened the demise of these traditions. Today people have too many outside commitments, and spend more hours at work. The guthi system is in decline.

In the Suburbs

Between Chhetrapati and Swayambhunath, down on the banks of the Vishnumati River, is a small temple dedicated to Shiva, called the **Indrayani** temple. Here are several erotic carvings, on the lower and upper levels. There are also some lingam-yoni stone images. Close by are two small delicately sculptured chaityas with the Dhyani Buddha figures on all four sides.

In the valley there are five main Tantric deities responsible for physio-psychic disorders. These are Harati, Bijeshwori, Bhat Bhateni, Unmatta Bhairab and a fifth one, Akash Bhairab, recognised only by Newaris.

Near the Indrayani temple, but across the river, are a couple of other temples. The **Bijeshwori** courtyard houses a three-tiered temple with some erotic art on display, as well as a fine Buddha. It is believed that the Bijeshwori temple, revered as Akash Yogini by Buddhists, may be a fifth Vajra Yogini. Upstream are the statues of the early democracy martyrs and the **Shova Bhagawati** temple. The deity is worshipped as one of the most powerful in the valley, as it can cause limb paralysis and weakness if offended. The idol is rumoured to have been carved by a sculptor with his feet, as he had no hands. A jealous King had his hands cut off to prevent him from reproducing an earlier masterpiece. Non Hindus cannot enter this white-walled complex.

In the **Bhat Bhateni** area is a small two-tiered temple with gilded roofs. Two dragon-like figures guard the Bhat Bhateni shrine. Here we find two large suspended idols, one red and the other yellow. These strange but large images are the couple deity held responsible for temporary limb paralysis, throbbing forehead and head pains. The torana has a three-faced image carrying a trident, which indicates the presence of the mixed deity, Mahakala/Bhairab, a Buddhist/Hindu deity. A large number of parasols crown the temple, one over the gajura itself.

In the small suburb of Naxal is a pond called **Nag Pokhari**, not far from the Royal Palace. Nag Pokhari has a gilded naga in the pond and a couple of small-modernised shrines. Some old houses grace the waterfront. The crumbling quadrangle nearby is called **Nandikeshwor**. It has a domed Shiva temple with a very large trident and an angry-looking Hanuman. Nowadays it houses a youth centre.

Continuing on, heading towards **Chabahil** and the airport, is a small temple at a crossroads, the **Bhagawati** temple, which has unusual paintings and frescoes, as well as an unusual white tiled background. One such painting of note shows a skeleton dancing. These skeletons appear on a number of temples and also appear as embracing male-female in some places. Legends say the two skeletons represent ascetics who were so deep in meditation that they did not notice their heads had been cut off. Above are a number of erotic poses, all located at the base of the struts. A particularly acrobatic pose is to be found on the east side, near the corner.

In Kamaladi north of the clock tower is a small shrine for **Hanuman**. He hasn't moved, but he once sat in a quiet street close to a bahal of old houses. At one time the few cars and many cycles used to head around the shrine on a detour to pay homage. Now the deity is enclosed in a cage and the traffic tears past on one side. Poor Hanuman is destined for an immortal life sat under clouds of fumes until the end of the Dark Ages. The other larger complex here is quite modern, but houses a magnificent golden chaitya with **Ganesh** as the main deity. Around this shrine are various images set in the walls and three impressive rat/shrew images. Close by is the parking area for the Seto Machhendranath chariot with its huge wheels.

In the eastern suburbs is an isolated temple devoted to **Maitidevi**, another mother goddess. The main temple is a single-storey squat brick structure with an abstract idol within. There are however two magnificent toranas depicting Ganesh and Kumar beside the central deity. Gilded birds adorn the gilded roof and in all ten superb lions stand guard. Five magnificent stone chaityas exhibiting the four Dhyani Buddhas stand in line at the front of the main shrine.

Tundikhel is the large open field east of New Road, with Kanti Path along its west side. Rani Pokhari is the large pool off Kanti Path and was built in 1670 by Pratap Malla for one of his wives who had lost a child. Also along Kanti Path is the temple of **Mahakala**, a Shiva/Bhairab shrine with a black image surrounded by gold-coloured decorations. Both Hindus and Buddhists revere Mahakala as a protective deity. Two intricate lion/dragons guard the temple.

On the east side of Tundikhel but north, closer to Durbar Marg, are the Clock Tower and the Durbar college buildings that were constructed for the education of the Rana offspring.

On the south side of **Tundikhel**, on the way to the Singha Durbar, is the **Bhadrakali** temple on a large roundabout. Marriages used to take place here. Bhadrakali is another goddess who is said to be the wife of the King Pachali. The King was also Bhairab, but used his powers to maintain a disguise. One day his curious wife saw his terrifying face and ran away, falling near to the place that is now the temple. A little south, on the main road to Kalimati, is a large **Jagannath** temple near the stadium.

Close to the post office is the tall minaret-like building called the **Bhimsen Tower**.

At the end of Durbar Marg is the **Royal Palace** of the present king, a modern, interestingly designed building set in a vast area of gardens.

A Coach Breaks Down; 1984

We had the misfortune to break down right in front of the Royal Palace in an overland coach we had driven from Delhi. The policemen here were not best pleased, and insisted it should be moved at once. But no amount of shouting was going to make that coach move.

It was inevitable that we would need help to push it, so all the smiling policemen came over and assisted. The coach started, but the policemen were left with grubby black marks on their brand new smart white gloves. They were not smiling now. We shouted our thanks and drove off as quickly as possible.

They never got our number, thanks to the gods.

Outside the Palace

The Rana Palaces

All of these palaces and houses were inspired by the visit of Jung Bahadur Rana to England and evoke neo-classical inspiration. Most have Greek-style columns and large rambling gardens. The most elaborate is the Singha Durbar, which was partially destroyed by fire in 1974. It still houses the parliament and government offices, but is a shadow of its former glory. Chandra Shumsher Rana built it in 1901, with 17 courtyards; much of the materials were imported from Europe. The Ranas sold the Singha Durbar to the state, raising untold wealth. The Ranas were of course the state at that time. They then built many more grandiose palaces.

The **Hotel Shanker** up in Lazimpat is one fine example. The Lal Durbar section of the **Yak and Yeti** Hotel is another superb example of Rana building. It was once much larger. North of the current Royal Palace, beyond Gauridhara and Naxal, around Tangal, are three more examples including the **Tangal Durbar**. The Nepal Rastra Bank is housed in at least two such palaces in the Bhat Bhateni area and Tripureshwar.

Narayanihity is the name of the Royal Palace, but it is also the name of a deep sunken tank on the opposite side of the road. Part of the original palace building remains in the form of an elaborate old gate; this is a fine example of early Rana designs. The gate is near the cinema, towards Naxal.

131

The **Kaiser Library** (Keshar Mahal) is another such building, which is open to the public. Inside the rambling gardens, high trees are home to large colonies of bats. The 'Garden of Dreams' is now being renovated. The restoration of the garden area of the Kaiser Library is being funded by the Austrian Government in association with one of the Nepal Heritage committees. Elegant and finely restored pavilions surround well-maintained lawns, trees, flowerbeds and ponds. Soon it will be open to visitors, with restaurants, cafés and resting places where you can escape from the noise and fumes of the city traffic, withdraw from the hustle and bustle of Thamel, and find peace in a quiet corner of this beautiful garden. A booklet explains the history and plans for the development of this land, and shows the previous extent of the property, which reached as far as the Malla Hotel and to the edge of Thamel many years ago.

On entering the library building, you will be greeted by a snarling stuffed tiger, followed by two shiny suits of armour. Further in are a rhino skull, two globes, and a wild buffalo head sticking out of the wall as though to attack intruders. Up the staircase, on the left is a magnificent room with huge oil paintings of the Ranas and Kings Mahendra and Tribhuvan. The door to this room may be locked, but if you have an opportunity it is well worth entering. Grand chandeliers adorn the ceilings. In the centre is a line of interesting circular chairs, each with four outward-facing seats. At the far end is another room with a tiger rug and a sloth bear rug, both with the heads still attached and with the teeth still snarling viciously.

In the main library, the bookshelves are a dream; full of first editions and autographed copies of ancient books that one hardly dares look at, let alone touch. A fascinating place to visit for a few hours.

Rana palaces and houses are absolutely everywhere, in different states of decay.

Development of the City

There are quite a number of small temples, shrines and chaityas to be found all over the city, many being engulfed by modern buildings. New buildings, constructed mainly in the late eighties and early nineties, have replaced the old Newari houses of Dilli Bazaar and Bagh Bazaar. The narrow lanes behind the Royal Palace went at the same time, not coincidentally at the same time as an international SAARC summit was taking place.

The road from the Palace up through Lazimpat to Maharajganj and beyond to the ring road once had chickens, pigs and old houses dotted all
the way along. The city limits in 1974 extended little beyond Teku in the
south, beyond old Thamel in the west. The Rastra Bank, an old Rana
palace in Tripureshwar, marked the eastern suburbs. The airport was well
out of town and the ring road did not exist then, being built a few years
later, but still remaining rural in character for several years.

Tea at the Hotel Shanker, 1980

*Today we marvel at the amazing computer technology
that gives us instant connections to the world from
Kathmandu. We may even complain about how slow
the e-mails are today, but only twenty years ago to get
any message out of the valley took an all-night phone
call or hours at one of the few telex machines.*

*There were many advantages to this state of affairs,
for one could never be contacted by head office in a
hurry and if the news was not to one's liking one could
deny having received the said message. It didn't always
work in our favour though, when funds were not
forthcoming.*

*One of the few such telex machines existed at the Hotel
Shanker, a fine edifice with a great tea lawn. (A Tiffin
lawn in earlier days, one suspects).*

*Working for a trekking company was a lot of fun in
those days; no one ever knew if clients would arrive
on time, or at all, or whether they would leave, for that
matter.*

*It has to be said though, that Royal Nepal Airlines was
rather good when it worked in those days.*

Dilli Bazaar, Kathmandu, January 1986

Two men come out of the dark and dingy room; they are chained together. A toilet along the balcony issues forth an unsavoury smell, a smell so familiar in these old government buildings. A plane overheard drowns out all conversation. The men look grim-faced; a judgement has been made. One can only assume that prison is the next stop.

We are near Dilli Bazaar on a cold wintry morning. The sun is just burning through a thick dew-laden fog. People are coming to work on their bicycles. We make our way through the whitewashed building with green windows, a long verandah on the ground floor and a long balcony on the first floor. Men in Nepali dress, white jodhpurs, dark European-style jackets and Nepali topi caps, congregate.

It is already eleven o'clock and no work has been done, save for that of the District Commissioner who has pronounced on the two men.

We go in to see him next.

After a few minutes and some ink rituals involving the placing of thumbprints on the paper, we are pronounced, in Nepali, to be married, we think.

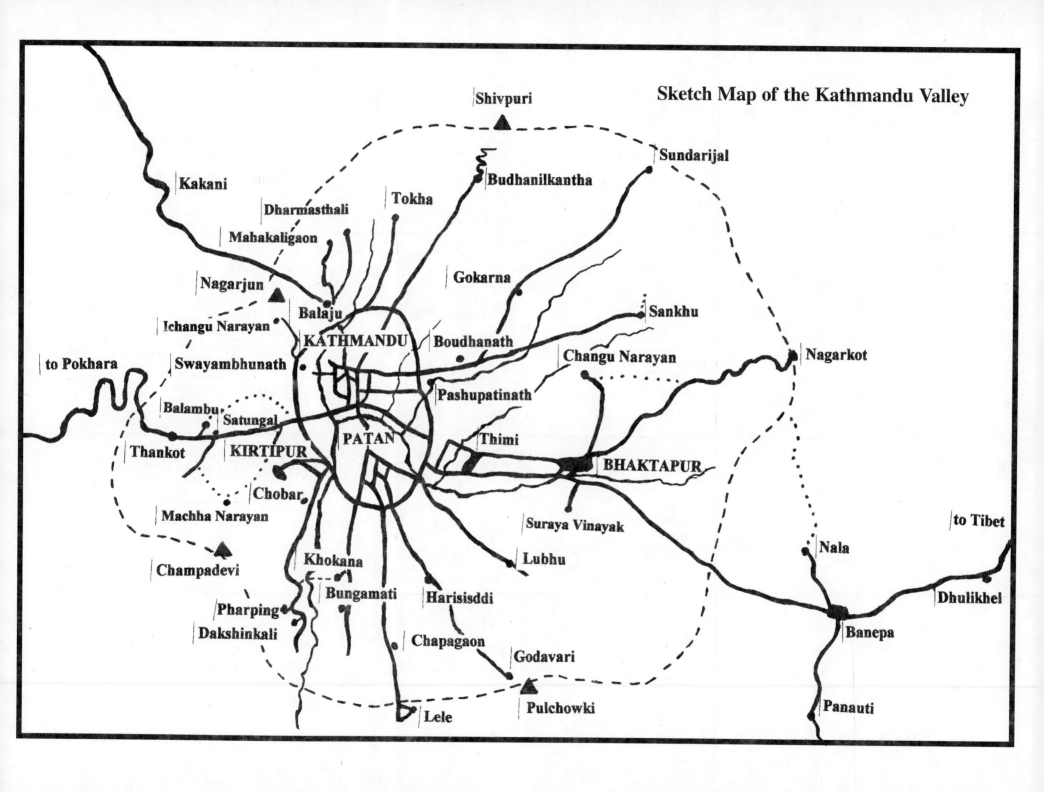

Sketch Map of the Kathmandu Valley

Shivpuri

Kakani

Budhanilkantha

Dharmasthali

Tokha

Mahakaligaon

Sundarijal

Gokarna

Nagarjun

Sankhu

Balaju

Ichangu Narayan

KATHMANDU

Boudhanath

Changu Narayan

Nagarkot

to Pokhara

Swayambhunath

Pashupatinath

Balambu

Satungal

Thimi

Thankot

KIRTIPUR

PATAN

BHAKTAPUR

Chobar

Suraya Vinayak

to Tibet

Machha Narayan

Lubhu

Nala

Champadevi

Khokana

Harisisddi

Dhulikhel

Pharping

Bungamati

Dakshinkali

Chapagaon

Banepa

Godavari

Lele

Pulchowki

Panauti

CHAPTER EIGHT
To the North of Kathmandu

Budhanilkantha

Budhanilkantha is the home of the famous reclining or sleeping Vishnu, upon whose image the Kings of Nepal may not look. The god rests on a bed of nagas (snakes). Vishnu is also known as Jalasayana Narayan here. To Buddhists he is Buddha Nilkantha or Nilkantha Lokeshvara, a form of Avalokiteshvara. Strangely, to Hindus he is 'old blue throat'. Blue is more often associated with Shiva, although Krishna, an avatar of Vishnu, is often blue. There are thought to have been four such idols at one time, though only three remain. The other two are within the Hanuman Dhoka palace gardens and at Balaju.

The huge black stone image is 6 metres long and probably dates from around 650 AD. Only Brahmins may stand on the idol. It is the largest stone sculpture in the valley and went missing after the Licchavi period. It was dug up during the time of Pratap Malla. He holds the four symbols of Vishnu in his hands. The Haribodhini festival is the main function at this shrine, although devotees come all year round.

With the opening of the Park Village Resort here, it is now possible to enjoy the tranquillity of the lower reaches of the Shivapuri National Park and the surrounding farming countryside without returning immediately to Kathmandu.

Tokha

North of Kathmandu, on the edge of the valley, is the ancient village of Tokha, said to be 2000 years old. Modernisation is rapidly overtaking Tokha, though there are still some interesting traditional houses in this village and an attractive small temple at the far end. There are no erotic carvings here. However, just at the entrance to the village is a beautifully carved and decorated Chaturmukha lingam-yoni with heads on each side, situated in the middle of a pond.

135

Valley scene near Tokha

Mahakaligaon and Dharmasthali

These two villages are rarely visited, but both are set in very pleasant rural settings just north of Balaju. A gentle three to three and a half hour trek can be made to these villages, starting from the new cinema north of Balaju, where the road goes to Nagarjun and further to Kakani and Langtang. You will need a map; the 'Nepa Maps' Kathmandu Valley edition shows the tracks. From the main road junction where the taxis and buses mainly stop, head downhill past a military area on the left and over the Mahadev Khola, then turn left. Cross the next bridge then go right, and then left up the hill, following a quiet country track. After Baniyagaon go down the track to the right into fields and bamboo forests, a particularly pleasant area. This track leads to Mahakaligaon. The temple is set on the highest hill; go up through the village and then up a steep path beside the school above the village.

The temple here is modern, but the attractions are the various stone-carved statues, idols and the views of the valley and northern hills. The main idol is a marble image of the goddess Mahakali Mai, one of the mother goddesses. There is a Shiva lingam within the temple and outside are a collection of rock lingams, tridents, Nandi bulls and a four-faced Chaturmukha lingam. To the south are several other stone images; one of Rama and Sita with an old and a newer Hanuman outside, and one of Krishna and Radha. On the east side is a magnificent image of Surya. Also within the complex on the west side is a small but intricate sleeping Vishnu and a colourful black stone Ganesh.

To go to Dharmasthali, follow the stepped stone pathway down, and continue through the farmhouses and bamboo clumps to a chataura, a porter's rest stop. Take the path down then head right to a small bridge over a stream; the dhobi ladies will probably be washing clothes here. Follow the wide dusty track down to a fork and take the road left uphill to Dharmasthali. This village has retained much of its rural farming atmosphere, although new houses are being constructed. A small stupa, with the four Dhyani directional Buddhas, is on the left at the entry to the village. As you continue on there is another stupa on the right and a small Ganesh shrine before the main square. Corn and wheat are dried in the square around two small shrines. The people seem genuinely friendly and certainly see few visitors. The scenery around this hilltop village is very charming and unchanged.

To return to Balaju, go back down the hill and continue ahead south along the valley, passing a number of new schools.

Kakani

This village is a viewpoint to the northwest, on the rim of the valley along the road from Balaju to the Langtang region. Views here are of Ganesh Himal, Himalchuli and the Gosainkund ridge.

Dhum Varahi

CHAPTER NINE
To the East of Kathmandu

We will first go in a northeast direction from the city.

Chabahil

Chabahil was once a separate village between Kathmandu and Boudhanath. Chabahil was prominent in the 6th and 7th centuries and the **stupa** is believed to have been founded by Ashoka's daughter. The stupa is much smaller than Boudhanath, with detailed chaityas grouped around the central shrine. Four Dhyani Buddhas face the cardinal points. To the north of the stupas is a small building, a gompa, which houses a repainted, black stone image of Shakyamuni Buddha. It is at least a thousand years old and may be as old as the 6th century. There is a brightly painted image of the green Tara on the left, as well as smaller images of Jambhala and Guru Rinpoche.

Just north of the stupa, in a crowded atmospheric bazaar, is one of the four main Ganesh shrines of the valley, **Chandra Vinayak**. It is busy with devotees. The black image of Ganesh sits below a gilded torana. Above the main portal of the idol is another fine torana. A wooden torana can be seen on the east side of this two-tiered temple. Ganesh here is a gatekeeper for Pashupatinath. The gilded vehicle of Ganesh, the rat, is standing on top of a column. Krishna is found in the building on the west side, playing his flute. The life-size idol lying down, but face up, is said by local people to be a Bhairab.

Dhum Varahi

This is one of the oldest shrines of the valley. The image is secured behind a marble entrance gate in a red brick structure, beneath and within a massive pipal tree. Here is the 6th century sculpture of Vishnu as a boar. The head faces left and it holds a deity in its left hand. The body is brightly coloured with vermilion powder and at the feet is another image. Two ancient lions guard the shrine, which is near a school. Some modern development now engulfs this once-rural shrine, but it still has a quiet and partially open location.

To reach it from the Boudhanath road, head north, downhill, on the ring road, cross the Dhobi Khola River and see a cinema on the right. About 100 m along on the left is a small lane that leads to this shrine.

Ram Mandir

This unusual temple is located in the Battisputali area of Kathmandu, not far from Pashupatinath and south of the Chabahil stupa. It is close to Dwarika's Hotel, a deluxe hotel that has been built in Newari style using old woodcarvings. Traditional methods have been used to create a heritage hotel with an amazing atmosphere of times long past.

The temple was built in 1871 during the period of Rana rule. It was built by Sanak Simha Lahuri Tandan Chhetri, whose name means old loyal lion. His sister was the favourite wife of Jung Bahadur Rana, the Prime Minister. A number of very large and elaborate Rana palaces were also built close by near the Bagmati river, but most of these have fallen into disrepair or been completely demolished.

The recently restored Ram Mandir can be accessed from a lane almost opposite the Dwarika hotel gate. Go down the lane for a few minutes, then climb a small hill by way of the temple stairway. Hanuman, a fine figure draped in red, greets the visitor and faces the main temple to the west. This temple complex is a mix of traditional Newari and Indian Moghul styles.

Inside the main sanctum are five images. The figures are made of black stone, with silver-coloured crowns and seven guarding golden snakes/*nagas* above each head. In the centre is Ram, more commonly known as Rama, the Hindu god made famous by the great Indian epic the Ramayana. To his left are his consort, Sita, and Laxman. To his right are Bharat and Satrughna.

The inside is a mix of large mirrors and murals. Non-Hindus may not enter, but if the lights are on, you can easily peer in to see the fine paintings above. These depict gods and saints, and many of the butterfly figures that give the area, Battisputali, its name, which means thirty-two (*battis*) butterflies (*putali*).

Around the temple are two restored *pathis*, long Newari brick buildings for offices and pilgrims to rest in, as well as a *sattal*, open shelter, on the north side. The nine square temples surrounding the main part are Shiva temples with lingams inside and stone-carved Kirtimukha/Chepu guardians above the main openings. The whole complex has a pleasant view west over the city and the mountains behind, particularly good since it is on the edge of a hillside.

Pashupatinath

On the banks of the holy Bagmati river is the Pashupatinath temple complex, so important to the Nepalese people. It is some five kilometres northeast of Kathmandu. Pashupatinath is the lord and protector of beasts and is the divine protector of Nepal. Deopatan was an area west of Pashupati and is now cut by the ring road.

There is evidence to suggest that the site has been in use since the Licchavi period, but it is since the 7th century that worship of Pashupati began in the valley. The ghats at Pashupatinath have become the most important in the valley; most days one can observe the cremation of the dead. The bodies are wrapped in cloth and placed on the plinths. The eldest son normally performs the act of lighting the fire. The women normally stay at home, but previously the wives used to perform suttee (sati), throwing themselves on to their husbands' pyres. The ashes are later swept into the holy Bagmati and flow down to the Ganges, giving the soul a direct passage out of the cycle of rebirth. Although a mere trickle for much of the year, a ritual bathe in the holy waters is assumed to give one great merit. It will allow one to go directly to Shiva's paradise on Mount Kailash. It might be a touch colder there!

On the ring road is a temple called **Jaya Bageshwari**, which once probably marked the western edge of the original area. This shrine was where widows performing suttee would pay homage before the ritual self-immolation. This three-tiered temple has an interesting wall mural painted in bright colours, showing dismembered bodies being carried by skeletons, for example. The central figure is the blue Bhairab Akash. A peacock and a lion on columns guard the west side. This tantric temple also offers fine strut carvings; some are erotic. It has a fine torana and images of the goddesses.

Entering the Pashupatinath complex from the ring road on the west, you pass a Kumar temple and then come down to the trinket sellers' area.

On the right are a number of pilgrims rest centres and the large Pancha Dewal with its Moghul-style domes. On the north side of the main entry road, go left to find the main temple area. A large gate marks the entrance with Shiva and his two sons, Ganesh and Kumar, displayed. Ganesh is on the left with the moon god Soma above. On the right is Kumar, with the sun god Surya above. Shiva stands central above them all.

There are different legends attached to Pashupatinath. In one tale, the sky god, Prajapati is copulating with his daughter Ushas, a dawn goddess, in the forest here. Rudra, the early name for Shiva, assumed his wild hunting aspect, Mahadev, and interrupted this nefarious activity, shooting Prajapati with an arrow. Instantly a lingam arose and so we have Pashupatinath. Sadhus, aesthetics, yogis and holy men regard Mahadev as their main deity.

The Shiva temple complex at Pashupatinath is off limits to non-Hindus, but you can peer through the doorway on the west side. There is a view of the rear end of a large Nandi bull, the vehicle for Shiva. To see the rest of his magnificent golden figure, you will have to climb up the steps on your left, go round to the right past the rest houses, and peer down over the wall. But be discreet and respectful.

The main temple contains the sacred Shiva lingam. It is apparently one metre high, set in black stone with faces at each corner and an imaginary fifth face looking to the sky. These faces are believed to be Shiva, Surya, Vishnu and Buddha. The main gold temple stands on the site of earlier shrines and was built in the 17th century. The temple complex can be viewed from the other side of the river from an area high up below the forest canopy. Steps lead up here, past many small shrines and a fair few sadhu holy men. Monkeys abound here; be careful!

Tantric practices were once more popular than today, but there is some evidence to be found just down by the bridge across the river. Open to the non-Hindu public, is a small Shiva temple, the **Bachaleshvari** temple. Here on the struts are erotic carvings, recently painted in silver with images on the main walls behind them. One image is of a skeleton in black and white. A seven-headed serpent hangs above a red image of the Buddha next to this temple. This is an image of the Dhyani Buddha, Amoghasiddhi. Buddhists regard Pashupati as Avalokiteshvara, but the whole shrine complex is fundamentally Hindu.

Apart from all the Shiva lingams and yonis in the area east of the river, up in the forest, there are few erotic carvings at Pashupatinath. Across the river on the right are eleven chaityas and their lingams dedicated to the women who performed suttee. Suttee is now forbidden, although it still happens on occasion in rural India.

Heading south from the main area along the river on the west bank after the cremation ghats, one finds an **enormous lingam** said to be more than 1500 years old. The yoni is over a metre across, and the lingam is very large indeed. A serene-looking statue of the **Buddha**, said to be 6th – 7th century, a little out of place, stands close by, not knowing what to make of the scene. Some say it is an image of Vishnu's tenth avatar, Kalki who will arise after the age of Kali finishes. The **Raj Rajeshwari** is a rounded temple with a bull, the trident and a bell on three sides. In the same courtyard is an exquisite gilded single-tiered temple dedicated to the nine Durgas, who can be seen inside garlanded with skulls. This is the **Nawa Durga** temple. Eyes and some erotic figures appear on the temple.

Retracing your steps now to the main bridge, you begin the climb into the **Mrigasthali**, deer forest, an extensive woodland area, but beware of the monkeys. As you climb up here, you will often find many sadhus resting in the complex on the right. There are a couple of shrines here dedicated to Vishnu as **Lakshmi Narayan** and **Ram**, Vishnu's mortal being and hero of the Ramayana. His wife **Sita** was rescued from Ravena, the demon of Sri Lanka. Sita was born in Janakpur, where the Janaki temple is an almost whimsically proportioned Moghul-style palace.

Up the stairway at the top and to the left beyond the orange Ganesh image is a complex of chaityas, more yonis and lingams and the shikhara-style **Gorakhnath** temple. This area was restored in 2001-2002. Further east is another large quadrangle and temple with a dome-like centre; this too has been restored. This is the **Vishvarupa Mandir**, a Vishnu temple. Entry to non-Hindus is forbidden. There is a Hanuman image and three bells visible, but the erotic vision of Shiva and Shakti that is said to be here cannot be seen.

On the northern edge of the forest at the **Kirateshwari** temple is a massive red stone lingam. Down the steep steps go left, and near the bridge over the Bagmati are some more lingams by the ghat here. It is a quiet forested riverside spot. A path from here leads uphill via the Kailash hillock to the main temple gate; full circle. From the hill another path leads down to the hermit caves by the riverside.

From the bridge follow the paved walkway to the east. Along here is the **Gujeshwari** temple, the female link with Pashupatinath. The mysterious goddess Gujeshwari is another aspect of Durga, Kali and Taleju, whose powers are so dreadful they must be hidden. The temple is the sacred bottomless hole where Gujeshwari resides. One can just see the four Naga serpents that stand above the shrine from a path above the temple in the forest. There are various legends about this shrine, most involving the corpse of Shiva's consort Sati, who immolated herself over an insult to Shiva. Her most sacred bits of body came to rest deep here where the shrine is located.

Gujeshwari is also sacred to Buddhists, for this is the place where a divine lotus took root below the mythical lake of Kathmandu. This is the same lotus that floated on the lake to become Swayambhunath. Buddhists also consider this place to be one of the homes of the four mystical Vajra Yoginis, the powerful tantric goddesses. Gujeshwari is thus linked to Tantra, the Adi Buddha and Swayambhunath.

The Sadhus of Pashupatinath

Here we happily digress once more and delve into the world of the holy men, the sadhus who live and display their talents at Pashupatinath, the location of so many stone erotica.

The sadhus are holy men who believe that human salvation lies only in renouncing the temptations of the material world. (Difficult!) They subscribe to an ancient religious philosophic system, Vedic Hinduism, dating from more than 3000 years ago. "Sadhu" is a word as old as Sanskrit itself. In the first of the four Veda texts, "sadhu" denoted "that which reaches the goal unerringly." Now it is more commonly used to mean a man who is endowed with spiritual learning, has high religious values and is virtuous in thought, word and deed.

On joining a Shiva sect at Pashupatinath, a sadhu renounces all connections with his family. His worldly life is at an end - he offers prayers, along with forty-eight balls of wheat-flour dough, to the souls of his ancestors. This is his funeral, for when he dies, no rites

Pashupatinath

need to be performed. His body may be burned or cast into a river, preferably the holy Ganges. At Pashupatinath, the holy river is the Bagmati, which flows eventually into the Ganges.

Some sadhus adhering to the Shiva sect lead itinerant lives, to prevent them from becoming attached to anything. They never spend more than three days in any one place. Some other sadhus, however, live a sedentary life, out in the wilds, far from human habitation. They exist in caves high in the Himalayas, surviving on the fruits of the forest, sometimes maintaining a vow of silence for many years, if not the rest of their lives.

The more extreme Naga sadhus have no hair at all on any part of their bodies. They cover their bodies with a mixture of ash and sandalwood, which is a natural antiseptic and protects them from heat and cold. They serve the people as mentors and philosophers, and are able to give them advice on both personal and family problems, from a detached viewpoint.

Some of the sadhus at Pashupatinath have devised a novel way of extracting donations from curious tourists, by demonstrating their prowess at weightlifting with a somewhat excruciating yoga exercise!

No pictures are available in this book; we leave it to your imagination!

From Pashupatinath it is but a twenty-minute walk from Gujeshwari to Boudhanath. Take the small steel bridge over the Bagmati River and head northeast to join the main Boudhanath road a little to the east of the main south gate of the Stupa.

Sketch Map of Pashupatinath & Boudhanath

Key to Sketch Map of Pashupatinath & Boudhanath

1	Panch Dewal	6	Raj Rajeshwari
2	Bachaleshvari temple	7	Nawa Durga
3	Eleven Chaityas	8	Vishnu and Ram temples
4	Large lingam & yoni	9	Chandra Vinayak
5	Buddha statue		

Buddhist Prayer Wheel

Boudhanath

If you are tiring or feeling in need of release from the tensions of the erotic displays, then the delightful atmosphere of Boudhanath is for you. This is the centre for Tibetan Buddhist culture. Pilgrims and devotees walk clockwise, turning prayer wheels, around the base of the giant, all-seeing-eyed stupa. This is a distraction of a very relaxing nature. Evocative chants of Tibet sing out across the magical scene. Sweet incense and the soothing aroma of burning juniper fill the air. Time stands still.

Boudhanath has a number of rooftop cafés from where you can observe the scenes in comfort. The 'View Himalayan' Restaurant has the

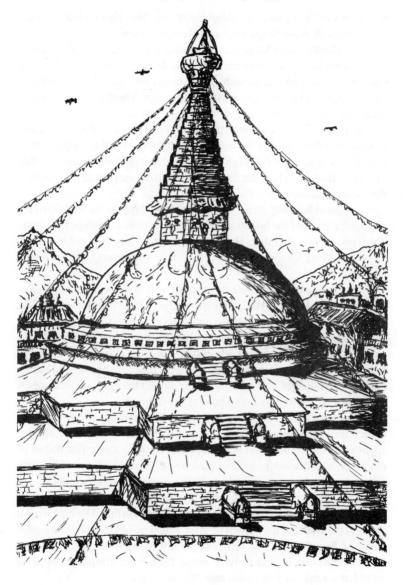

Boudhanath

best views of the mountains. Hotel Padma has the 'Festive Fare' restaurant, while others are Stupa View and Heavenly View.

The **Boudhanath Stupa** sits on squared plinths set in each direction, plus squares between. There are three base levels. On the east side of the main dome are a cluster of stupas. The larger one has Dhyani Buddhas. The smaller one has only one west-facing image. There are mini stupas at each of the four corners.

Assuming one enters from the south, head left and therefore clockwise around the stupa. On the west side of the stupa is a **Sakya-pa** monastery with a large thirty feet high image of Maitreya, the Buddha to come, the future Buddha. There are four figures on main entry wall representing the 'four directions,' Jambhala is one.

In a small building on the north side of the stupa are the images of the Tibetan deities and the bodhisattvas. Hundreds of butter lamps burn here; it's a mysterious chamber. Here you will find Guru Rinpoche (Padma Sambhava) and Chenresig (also called Avalokiteshvara), but no erotic embraces.

Attached to the stupa base on the north side is the **Ajima** temple. The image inside is Hariti or Harati, a silver image with no eyes in sockets. She is one of the mother goddesses also known to Tibetans as Jadzimo. Jadzimo is the female devotee who Tibetans believe began the building of the stupa. There is a large prayer wheel here. One can climb on to the stupa from here, passing two stone elephants with probably Mongolian riders. Note the 108 images of the bodhisattvas around the base of the dome. A new monastery is slowly being built at the north gate.

There is a legend about the origins of Boudhanath as follows. Once upon a time there was a King of Nepal who built a three-dragon-headed spout near Narayanhity, but no water came forth, so a sacrifice had to be made. He told his son to behead the body of a man under a white cloth near the spout. The prince carried out the sacrifice, but was shocked and grief-stricken to see it was his father's head he had cut off. He became a hermit at Vajra Yogini. The goddess here told the son that if he built a great stupa to the Buddha, his burden of grief would be lifted. And so the great stupa of Boudhanath was built. There are many other legends about Boudhanath; one is said to have come from Guru Rinpoche / Padma Sambhava. Links to Tibet were and still are strong.

In early spring at the Losar festival you are liable to cross paths, going clockwise around the stupa, with Sherpas, Tibetans, Khampas from eastern Tibet, and people from Dolpo and the mountains of north-western

Nepal. There are many new monasteries to the north of the stupa, including **Kopan** on the distant hillside. All the Tibetan Buddhist sects, Gelug-pa, Nyingma-pa, Sakya-pa and Kagyu-pa, as well as the Karma-pa, are represented here. There has been an incredible amount of building all around here. The abbot of **Ka Nying Shedrupling** monastery is Chokyi Nyima, who has become very well-known for his teachings to westerners studying Buddhism here.

In 1974 and until the mid-eighties there was little here but the stupa and its encircling quaint old houses. Fortunately the atmosphere remains intact, and one of peace.

Gokarna

Gokarna, located east of Boudhanath, is on the edge of the forest where the Bagmati River cuts through a narrow defile. Here is the temple of **Gokarneswari Mahadev**. It is an important Shiva shrine, and was restored in the early eighties by UNESCO. The festival of Gokarna Aunsi takes place here. The origins of Shiva worship may be traced to a legend associated with Gokarna. Shiva is said to have come to Pashupati deer forest as a gazelle. But Vishnu and Brahma wanted to take him back to Benares. In doing so they broke a horn off the gazelle, and a third of it landed at Gokarna.

A well-defined Hanuman image welcomes you to the site. The three-tiered temple has some amazingly detailed woodwork, including some chain links. Three doors are found on each side, with a single gilded torana facing east. Shiva, Parvati and their two sons, Ganesh and Kumar are shown here. Also within the temple is said to be a nude image of Shiva with an erection! The Gokarneswari lingam is said to be a stone with milk dripping on to it. All around the base of the main shrine are stone-sculpted images as well as lingams, another Hanuman image facing the river and a suckling cow on the upper west side called **Karmadhuti**. An ancient black image of Parvati is enshrined in the small temple close to the main edifice.

Down near the ghat is a small, rather skeletal, version of Vishnu reclining on some nagas. The unusual open wood pillared building here by the ghat is the **Vishnu Paduka** temple.

Sankhu

Sankhu is some 20 kilometres east of Kathmandu. The drive out is pleasantly rural, passing a new monastery on the left, and near Mulpani you may see (rice) paper drying in the sun. The village of Karthalitar remains little changed, with some traditional red/orange coloured farmhouses around about. Sankhu itself has been somewhat modernised along the main road, but further away, particularly on the northeast side, are some old bahals and traditional streets. There are still some very fine wooden windows on traditional houses within the town and a couple of very large pipal trees. Padma Sambhava is reputed to have stayed here in the late eighth century.

Just north of Sankhu is the famous temple of **Vajra Yogini**. To reach it from Sankhu on foot will take up to an hour, but by going part way on a rough road, you can start the climb from a teahouse. A well-maintained stone stairway leads up from here and the town. On the way you pass some waterspouts and a set of deities including a pot-bellied stone **Ganesh**, one of the best in the valley. He carries an axe and has four arms. A crown is on his head. The large triangular rock image represents **Bhairab**, and this is where the only blood sacrifices occur at this complex. A festival is held on the March-April full moon.

A few minutes up the path is the courtyard complex, **Gum Bahal**, with the three-tiered, gilded-roofed temple of Vajra Yogini, another of the tantric shrines devoted to the wrathful female aspect of Buddha. It was Vajra Yogini who is said to have asked Manjushri to cut open the Chobar Gorge. There is evidence to suggest that the Licchavis first used this place as a holy site. The main temple is surrounded by three waterspouts, many small chaityas and stupas, one of which is square. An unusual pataka runs down from the magnificent bell-shaped gajura on top of the pagoda.

Here at Sankhu, Vajra Yogini is a version known as **Ugratara**, and is the fearsome version of Tara. Here though she is not displayed in fearsome mood. The Sankhu Vajra Yogini is the eldest of the four Yoginis of the valley. She is called the Khadga Yogini. The Khadga is the sword she holds. The others are at Gujeshwori, Pharping (Phamthing) and Vidyeshvari. Some say another resides in Pulchowk in Patan.

The temple faces south, with a very detailed gilded torana above the door. It is one of the best in the valley. Here we see the main deity Vajra Yogini with smaller versions on either side; images of Baghini, a tiger Yogini, and Singhini, a lion Yogini. Vajrasattva and Vajradhara are above. There are protectors with long trunks about to devour Buddha images. Mermaid-like figures are shrouded by five nagas and at each side are three-headed images standing on bodies. A demonic bird-like Yogini stands sentinel above all this. If the doors are open, one can peer in, but only from the courtyard. The idol of Vajra Yogini is red here, and sits below an amazingly large golden-arched surround with seven nagas sitting at the top.

In the same courtyard is a smaller **two-tiered temple** containing a gilded stupa similar to that of Swayambhu. The eyes are more slanted though. On each side of the temple on the first level are intricately carved window panels with the Dhyani Buddhas in residence. Above the main door is an amazingly intricate tiny golden three-faced image.

Continuing up the stairs behind the main temples, we come to a large open courtyard with a number of pilgrims rest places and a central sunken bath. On the south side is the building which houses the **Buddha Mata** or **King Vikramajit**. Inside the main area is a large painted formerly gilded Buddha head—Buddha Mata—stuck in the floor, and another gilded stupa. A large upside-down metal cooking pot also sits here. As you go back down, on the left (east) side is a small building, which is home to the monks. A small image of the sixth Dhyani Buddha, **Vajrasattva** is kept here.

The whole area is very pleasant with plenty of shade in the forest. If you are trekking down from Nagarkot to Changu Narayan you may visit here. Keep an eye out for the monkeys in the forest.

Further East of Kathmandu

To reach Bhaktapur you must head out towards the airport and follow the ring road around to a junction. The road heading east leads to Bhaktapur, Thimi and Nagarkot, and then on to the border with Tibet. Now that the trolley bus is not running, the easiest way to Bhaktapur is by private taxi. Local buses are slow and crowded, but a reasonable alternative on the way back.

Bhaktapur

Bhaktapur is the third city of the valley and the one least affected by modern construction. It is also believed to be the oldest city in the valley, dating back to the Licchavi period mentioned earlier.

Bhaktapur, once a walled city, was the capital of the valley until invaders came from Gorkha. At one time shrines to the eight Matrika goddesses were found around its corners for divine protection. Many of its finest structures were lost in the great earthquake of 1934. Some further damage

Sketch Map of Bhaktapur Durbar Square

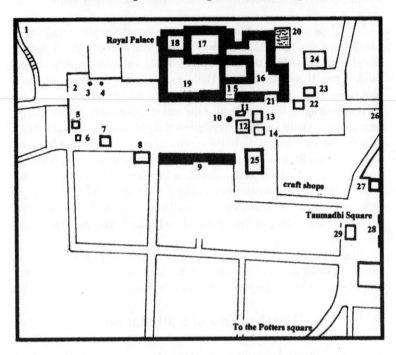

Key to Sketch Map of Bhaktapur Durbar Square

1	Bus park entry	9	New café and Durga shrine
2	Entrance gate	10	Bhupatindra Malla column
3	Bhairab statue	11	Taleju bell
4	Durga statue	12	Vatsala Durga temple
5	Jagannath shrine	13	Chyasilin temple
6	Rameshwar shrine	14	Sunken bath
7	Bansi Narayan temple	15	Sun Dhoka gate
8	Shiva shikara	16	Bhairab Chowk

17	Mul Chowk	24	Shiva temple
18	Kumari Chowk	25	Pashupatinath temple
19	National Art Gallery	26	To Tadhichhen Bahal
20	Nag Pokhari	27	Nyatapola temple
21	Palace of 55 Windows	28	Bhairabnath temple
22	Siddhi Lakshmi shikara	29	Café Nyatapola
23	Bhadrakali-Durga temple		

occurred in 1988, again due to a smaller earthquake that could be felt even in Thamel.

It was almost one hundred percent Newari and Hindu until recent development. Its people were once fiercely traditional; many still are. These days some of its inhabitants are extremely political in outlook. Bhaktapur has been designated a world heritage site. At one time its streets were host to huge amounts of organic waste, but that was all cleaned up by a German restoration project. Unfortunately this Teutonic cleanliness did not do the pigs that fed on the waste much good. The pigs retreated, but were reinstated later with proper arrangements. Today, though, the pigs are a rare sight. It is to be hoped that Bhaktapur will be allowed to retain its significant historic atmosphere. Some of the film Little Buddha was made here, and for one who knows the area it is amusing to see the Little Buddha fly from Boudhanath to Bhaktapur in an instant!

You can enter Bhaktapur from the new tourist Bus Park off the Nagarkot road. At one time people entered along the western roadway, through pleasant forest, passing the Na Pokhari, also called the Guhya pond. This road seems to be closed at times. Close to Durbar Square, on the west side before the entry gate, is the **Shiva-Parvati** temple with erotic art and erotic elephants.

Both ways lead to the gate at Durbar Square. **The entry fee for foreign tourists is US $10**.

The Durbar Square is the smallest of the three cities', being a shadow of its original size. However there are some gems within the square. On the right are some small shrines; one is devoted to Vishnu as Bansi Narayan, Krishna is its deity. The long brick and wood façade on the right was restored in 2001. The next temple is a Durga temple.

On the north side, left as you enter, are images of Bhairab and Durga. The main building is the national art gallery set in the Royal Palace. On a column sits **King Bhupatindra Malla**, Bhaktapur's most famous King. A **Taleju** bell is seen here, together with a smaller bell. Both sit here next to the stone temple known as **Vatsala Durga**. This was constructed by Bhupatindra Malla in the late 17th century and is similar to the **Krishna** temple in Patan. The newly rebuilt (1990s) **Chyasilin** temple, a very picturesque wooden structure, is located northeast of the Vatsala Durga temple.

The **Royal Palace** was once believed to have had nearly a hundred courtyards; now just six remain intact. Most of the remains date from the late 16th century. The magnificent **Golden Gate** is an astonishing masterpiece that many early visitors waxed lyrical about, including Perceval Landon, the explorer. Constructed in 1753, it is called the **Sun Dhoka**. Above the doorway is a golden embossed torana illustrating the deity Taleju with heads on two levels. The lower head has three faces. The Birdman protector sits above. Entering the complex, one comes to a narrow area called Beko or **Bhairab Chowk**. Next is the entrance to the **Taleju Chowk**, which cannot be entered by non-Hindus. Further inside are the **Mul Chowk** and the **Kumari Chowk**; both are off-limits. The sunken bath of **Nag Pokhari** is in the northeast corner, with little left except a fine spout and a gilded snake's head. Palace buildings must have surrounded this overgrown area once.

East of the Sun Dhoka is the **palace of fifty-five windows**. Only fifty-three remain. Built in 1697, this three-storied building has some fine carvings. The **Siddhi Lakshmi** shikara is the white temple. The **Bhagawati** temple is close by, another Durga shrine, and the Matrika goddesses are seen here. Some evidence of parts of the palace that were destroyed can also be seen.

Close to the Vatsala Durga temple is one of the most famous temples here, the **Pashupatinath** temple, dedicated to Shiva and built in around 1482 by Yaksha Malla. There are some interesting erotic carvings to be found on this temple. A small shrine to the goddess **Gujeshwari** is seen here.

One of the least visited shrines is the **Tadhichhen Bahal**. It is a Buddhist enclave and houses one of the few images of the bodhisattva Dipanker. This is found close to Durbar Square on the northeast side. Dipanker, the enlightener and an early disciple of Buddha, is the red Buddha wearing a crown. This little courtyard also has some amazing carvings; one shows two rams kissing a reticent figure, and another has two

Manjushri figures attacking a snake. Further along are some monkey men, and another figure has his teeth being pulled by pliers, presumably a newly constructed addition.

Pashupatinath Temple, Bhaktapur

Southeast of Durbar Square, down a narrow alley close to the Pashupatinath temple, is **Taumadhi Square**. The five-tiered **Nyatapola temple** is the most eye-catching structure and is one of the highest temples of all at 30 metres. Built by Bhupatindra Malla in 1702, the temple is dedicated to a goddess so powerful that her identity still remains uncertain. Many consider Siddhi Lakshmi to be that goddess. There are no erotic features on this temple, which is guarded by elephants, dragons and lions. Two mythical wrestlers Jai Mal and Patta stand at the base.

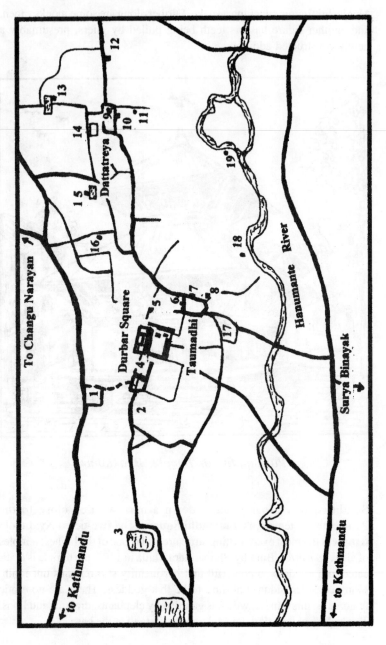

Sketch Map of Bhaktapur

Key to Sketch Map of Bhaktapur

1	Bus park	11	Peacock Window
2	Shiva Parvati temple	12	Wakupati temple
3	Na Pokhari	13	Nawa Durga temple
4	Durbar Square	14	Salna Ganesh temple
5	Tadhichhen Bahal	15	Nag Pokhari tank
6	Nyatapola temple	16	Mahakali Dyochhen
7	Bhairabnath temple	17	Potters' Square
8	Til Mahadev Narayan temple	18	Bhadrakali Pitha
9	Dattatreya temple	19	Hanuman Ghat
10	Pujari Math		

Across the square is the magnificent **Bhairabnath** temple, which was begun under Jagat Jyoti Malla and extended upwards later during Bhupatindra's rule. Bhairab's idol is paraded around the streets of the town during the Bisket festival of the New Year. Legends abound about this temple, sometimes known as Akash Bhairab. One legend connected to the temple tells how Bhairab came in human form to see the New Year Bisket festival. However, a Tantric sage saw him and tried to bind him with spells, but he got free. The Tantric cut off his head and enshrined it in the temple. In a different version, Bhairab was sinking into the ground to escape the Tantric's spell. Bhairab's consort as Bhadrakali saw the head of her husband and cut it off to preserve it and keep it with her at the temple.

Another legend says that when Bhupatindra Malla built on two extra storeys to the temple, the gods were enraged. Serious earthquakes followed later and, to appease Bhairab, the Nyatapola Mandir was built for Bhairab's consort Siddhi Lakshmi.

Adjacent to the south is the **Til Mahadev Narayan** temple with a lingam-yoni on display. It might have been founded as early as 1080. This structure probably dates back three hundred years or so. The temple exhibits icons and displays of Vishnu, but has the Shiva lingam.

Also in Taumadhi Square is the **Café Nyatapola** temple, now a pleasant tourist retreat above the busy square. Some erotic carvings may be viewed here at close quarters. The curries are hot stuff too!

From the square head east along the main thoroughfare for ten to fifteen minutes and you will reach the impressive **Dattatreya Square**. It is also called **Tachupal Tole** and is exceedingly picturesque. The central focus is the Dattatreya temple, which has been added to over the years, being originally constructed in a similar way to the Kasthamandap in Kathmandu. This temple is dedicated to the trinity, Vishnu, Shiva and Brahma. Dattatreya is a god who is more normally worshipped in southern India, and there is some mystery as to why this temple is to be found in Bhaktapur. Yaksha Malla built the temple we see today around 1427. Raja Viswa Malla also added to its splendour. It is one of the oldest temples in Bhaktapur. Carvings here appear on three sides, but not at the entrance on the west-facing side. Some are rounded with age, and this is believed to be one of the oldest temples in the whole of the Kathmandu valley. In front are the guardians, Jai Mal and Patta.

Most of the other buildings around the square were rest houses for pilgrims, sages and devotees. These are called Maths. The Maths are similar to the Bahals of Kathmandu. **Pujari Math** is the most significant, and was probably built around 1480. Today it is a woodcarving museum; the interior has some amazing carvings, including one of Bhairab. Nearby down a narrow lane is the famous **Peacock Window**, a delicately carved wooden masterpiece. On the west side of the square is a Bhimsen temple.

Continuing east, you will come to the **Wakupati** temple, which is devoted to Narayan as Vishnu. Here is an ornate lingam and yoni, as well as a fine gold conch. There are a couple of erotic poses on the north side of the temple. Vishnu holds his chakra here. Northwest of the Wakupati temple is the **Nawa Durga Dyochhen** shrine; this looks more like a normal house. The nine fearsome Durga deities here are important to the people of Bhaktapur. The Nawa Durga dancing troupe performs masked ritual tantric displays during festivals in the city.

On the north side of Dattatreya Square is a fine Buddha-headed lingam-yoni statue in the small dragon temple by the **Salan Ganesh** Lake. The next lake to the west is **Nag Pokhari**, with the naga, snake, sitting in the cool waters. On the **Thalachhen** temple nearby are further examples of simple erotic carvings. The next lake is **Bholachhen Pokhari**. Heading south now, you find the **Mahakali Dyochhen** temple with quite a number of excited figures high up. Two dragons guard this temple. Heading south brings us to the main street again.

Bhaktapur, Nyatapola Temple

South of Durbar Square is the animated **Potters' Square**, not to be missed; best for photography in the morning. A small Ganesh shrine is located here. There are a few other temples close to the Potter's Square built in the Dyochhen style. All along the south side of the main street are quiet residential streets full of daily life; the mysterious alleys and lanes that give Bhaktapur its medieval atmosphere.

Further south along the Hanumanta River, erotic carvings can be found on the small **Bhadrakali** temple, together with Ganesh and a snake god. Nearby are some stone lingam/yonis; eleven are found in the courtyard of the Shivalaya temple. A large lingam is also to be seen at **Hanuman Ghat**.

Thimi

Thimi is approximately three kilometres west of Bhaktapur. It is a farming town, also famous for its pottery and papier-mâché. Much of the town retains its traditional appeal, with many untouched side alleys. Some new structures have been built, with some in the old style. There are still an amazing number of elaborate old wooden windows. Entering this long town from the south, you come first to the **Bal Kumari** temple. Thimi has a Kumari, along with all the main towns of the valley. The Kumari must be worshipped, for she can give rains and good harvest, as well as fertility to young women. The Kumari attends the New Year festivities when people traditionally used to throw coloured dyes (see Festivals).

A wonderful gilded peacock stands high on a column at the front of the gilded, three-tiered temple; this is the vehicle of the goddess. There are six wooden toranas here, some with dog-like images holding snakes. The idol itself appears abstract and small. Inside the shrine is a square lingam with an image of the goddess on each of its four faces. The next temple heading north is the **Karunamaya**, Avalokiteshvara temple. There are 108 glass-covered images of Lokeshvara around the first level, as well as prayer wheels. A vajra sits on the north side and across the street is a magnificent window.

Continuing on, we reach a small brick shikhara temple and a Ganesh idol. Then we find a stupa next to a Garuda/Narayan shrine, a large pond, a small tank and a small shrine of Krishna with a flute in his hands. A helmeted Garuda is close by. The two-tiered temple next is a Bhairab place of worship, with a subsidiary gajura on top and some quite adventurous erotic depictions. Two lions guard the **Lyay Mha Pucha** (Bahal) with

Shakyamuni Buddha inside. After two small shrines we come to an impressive stupa with a mini Swayambhunath on top and eight subsidiary stupas. Unusually, a Hindu image sits at the west side. After this we reach the secondary road to Bhaktapur; beyond is new urban development and Bodegaon (Bode).

The three-tiered temple in **Nagdesh** village, adjacent to Thimi, is a temple devoted to Ganesh. King Nagaraja is the legendary founder of the village.

Bode

In this nearby village a strange ritual takes place (again see Festivals) when a chosen man parades about with an iron needle through his tongue and also carrying burning torches. It is a ritual which pays homage to the goddess Mahalakshmi and concludes at her shrine, where the man removes the iron needle and scrapes mud on to the wound to stop the bleeding. If this happens all is well, but if bleeding continues, it is a bad omen.

Surya Vinayak

This is one of the four main shrines in the valley devoted to Ganesh, and is on the south side of Bhaktapur up on the wooded hillside. It is east-facing and is the first place in the valley to catch the rays of the sun. Surya is the sun god, while Ganesh here is said to cure the deaf and the lame. Newly-wedded people come to get his blessings for a happy marriage and for children.

Steps lead up to the shrines. Kumar, Ganesh's brother, is found on his peacock vehicle here. The main temple is a shikhara-style building with an abstract stone image of Ganesh. Toranas arch over the image, with nagas prominent. Four gilded nagas hang down from the top. There is a large imposing rat or shrew here, mounted on a pillar.

Beyond Bhaktapur

Changu Narayan

Changu Narayan village and temple complex lies about seven kilometres north of Bhaktapur, and can most easily be reached by going north from

Bhaktapur on a reasonable road. It lies on the end of a ridge that extends east to Nagarkot, and it is possible to trek part way along the ridge up or down from Nagarkot. A couple of pleasant cafés exist here, and there is now a Rs. 60 entry fee for foreigners.

The temple complex is one of the oldest such structures in the valley and it is designated as a world heritage site. It is believed to date from the 4th century and has been reconstructed many times since. King Manadeva, a Licchavi monarch, is associated with the shrine. In earlier times the place was known as **Champakaranya**. The latest structure dates from 1702 and contains some of the finest woodwork, brickwork, carving and decoration done in the valley. The **Mila Punhi** festival centres on Changu Narayan.

Sketch Map of Changu Narayan

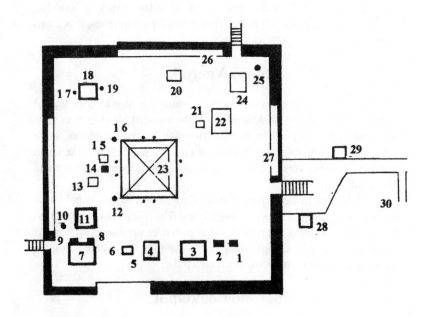

Key to Sketch Map of Changu Narayan

1	Ganesh shrine	16	Chakra on column
2	Elephant carving	17	Garuda Narayan image
3	Chinnamasta temple	18	Krishna temple
4	Badeshwar Mahadevi temple	19	Vishnu Sridhara sculpture
5	Vishnu Vaikuntha sculpture	20	Nateshwari shrine
6	Vishnu Vishvarupa sculpture	21	Vishnu Madhab
7	Lakshmi Narayan temple	22	Vishnu and Avalokiteshwara
8	Vishnu Vikranta sculpture	23	Main temple
9	Narasingha sculpture	24	Mahavishnu sculpture
10	Bhairab shrine	25	Shiva lingam
11	Kileshwar temple	26	Resthouse
12	Conch on column	27	Khat store
13	Bhupatindra Malla and wife	28	Bhimsen Pathi
14	Manadeva inscription stone	29	Balampu Pathi
		30	Open sky museum
15	Kneeling Garuda		

Changu Narayan is Lord Vishnu's main home in the valley; a home he took after killing an evil Brahmin and wandering in repentance. There are many differing legends associated with this site. For Hindus, Narayan is Vishnu. Buddhists know Narayan as Hari Hari Vahan Lokeshvara. Newari Buddhists believe a legend which says that Garuda, the sky god, was in conflict with the nagas and this stopped the rains. Avalokiteshvara came by and stopped the fighting. He put a naga around Garuda's neck. Vishnu then mounted Garuda and put Avalokiteshvara on his shoulder, bowing to his superior wisdom. Within the complex are many shrines and images depicting different aspects of Vishnu. Vishnu's vehicle Garuda is prominent.

Entering the courtyard from the village and walking clockwise, you will first see Ganesh and a sculpted elephant. Next is the 17th century temple of **Chinnamasta**. This small but brightly gilded temple is that of the beheaded Parvati, who according to Hindu mythology cut off her head to feed her hungry friends Saheli and Prakriti, and thus became Chinnamasta. It is said to contain twelve images, including those of the mother goddesses of the valley, the Astha Matrika/Harati/Ajima. Worship of the mother goddesses is believed to be older than worship of the Hindu trinity in its current form. A temple devoted to **Badeshwar Mahadevi** is close by.

Next we see the famous stone sculptures of Vishnu in different aspects. Facing east is a **Vishnu Vaikuntha** sculpture that relates to his Tantric aspect. Vaikuntha represents paradise for the fourteen-armed, seven-headed Narayan with Lakshmi on his knee. Lakshmi is his Shakti, giving him energy. Both are seated above a six-armed Garuda. On the other side is a partly broken image. This **Vishnu Vishvarupa** image dates from the 8/9th century and illustrates Vishnu in cosmic form. The ten-headed and ten-armed god is standing on the cosmic serpent, a serpent called Ananta who represents creation in an abstract form. The general scene is said to be an illustration from the Bhagavad Gita.

Vamana, the dwarf avatar and first human form, is the fifth aspect of Vishnu. The statue here is **Vishnu Vikranta**, the god who reclaimed the universe from the demon Bali by disguising himself as the dwarf. **Narasingha**, another Vishnu avatar, is seen disembowelling the demons in the next relief. These reliefs are set on the lower level of the **Lakshmi Narayan** temple.

Tucked away in this corner is a **Bhairab** image and here also is the **Kileshwar** temple, called by some the Pashupatinath shrine. It is the small two-tiered temple with a central four-faced chaturmukha lingam and some erotic figures on the lower part of the struts.

The **central two-storied pagoda** is one of the largest in the Kathmandu Valley. Inside the main shrine Vishnu rides Garuda, but non-Hindus may not enter. The temple has a gilded upper and a tiled lower roof. Ten manifestations of Vishnu are represented high on the roof struts. At the corners are the four symbols of Vishnu, the conch, wheel, lotus and the mace. Narayan is shown on the magnificent golden torana above the equally ornate gilded doors. Elephants, lions, griffins and sarduls (mythical manbird creatures) guard the four doors of the temple. Also in front of the main west-facing doors is a Licchavi period inscribed pillar dated as 464 AD. The kneeling 6th century Manadeva Garuda faces the temple and so do the gilded copper images of King Bhupatindra and his Queen. (Some scholars believe these figures to be Queen Riddilakshmi and her son, two 17th century benefactors).

Next along is a **Krishna** shrine with the Garuda Narayan image that appears on the Nepalese ten-rupee note. The next sculpture is of the **Sridhara Vishnu**, another 8/9th century image. Here we see Vishnu, Lakshmi and Garuda on pedestals. The **Nateshwari** shrine next is a Shiva Parvati place of devotion. Along this side of the courtyard is a pilgrim's rest house. Finally we come to the last corner in the northeast.

There are two raised plinths here next to a Vishnu image. One plinth here is kept for Vishnu and **Avalokiteshvara** or Padmapani, the only Buddhist deity in the complex. The other has the 16th century **Mahavishnu** sculpture. Narayan or Vishnu has ten arms and is with Lakshmi on his knee in cosmic pose. Both are seated above a six-armed Garuda. A Shiva lingam sits in the corner. Along the last wall here is a collection of khats, elaborate idol-carrying boxes, and a small chariot with carved wooden elephants above its wheels.

As you walk down through the village, you can visit the open sky museum, water spouts and tanks on the way to the car park. Changu Narayan can also be visited by climbing steeply up from the Manahara river, accessed from the Boudhanath to Sankhu road. There is no bridge, so wading across is the only option unless the river is too high.

Changu Narayan is one of four sites dedicated to Narayan or Vishnu in the valley. The others are Ichangu Narayan, Shesh Narayan and another, called Bisankhu Narayan, is near Bandegaon, beyond Harisiddhi. Some people add to these the Machha Narayan near Thankot as a fifth.

A Trek from Changu Narayan to Nagarkot

From the village car park of Changu Nararyan, follow the road uphill and through the picnic forest glade to the point where the road goes downhill to the right. Here you will see two tracks; take the one between the road and the one to the left, which goes up on to an open area. After a while you will pass the Changu Narayan Hill Resort and some houses. About fifteen minutes later you reach a village with a water tap. Go right here, uphill, with traditional farmhouses on your left. About fifteen minutes later, keeping to the wide track, you come to a zone of trees. There are two tracks here; taking the upper left one leads to some shrines and a nice view.

From the shrines you can cut down to the track you see below, but it is steep in places. Now you enter a very pleasant forested area for a further 15 minutes. After this you descend and take the left path when you see the main road below. It is about two hundred metres down to the road, which makes a tight hairpin turn here near some shops. This is the village of Telkot, and drinks can be bought here.

Now for simplicity it is easier to follow the main, but relatively quiet, tarmac road until you see a bus or any other likely transport; it is still 8 km to Nagarkot. It is said to be possible to continue uphill up the steep steps from the hairpin bend and, once on the ridge, to follow it up further to Nagarkot, but others have also found this hard to follow, and ended up lost. So don't try it unless you have lots of time and the weather is good!

Nagarkot

This village lies to the east of Kathmandu, on the edge of the valley rim. High on the ridge, above the smog of the city, the panoramic views from Everest in the east to Dhaulagiri in the west are superb. Looking north, we see the Himalayan peaks of Dorje Lakpa and Phurbi Chyachu. Further east is the spire of Chobha Bamare, then the twin-peaked summits of Gauri Shankar. Further east is Numbur, near Junbesi. Everest itself is just visible on a clear day, hidden behind the tangled knot of peaks of the upper Rolwaling valley, including Menlungtse, Pigperago and Pachermo.

A number of guesthouses and hotels are found here, catering to all budgets. The Club Himalaya is the top resort, with the popular Tea House nearby. Nagarkot is reached by road via Bhaktapur, or on foot via Changu Narayan. A three to four hour trek via the southern hill top links Nagarkot to Nala and Banepa, see below.

A Trek from Nagarkot to Banepa

From the Tea House in Nagarkot, follow the road south, climbing gently to the army camp. The road gets steeper on the way to a couple of new resorts before reaching another military zone. About one hour from Nagarkot you reach the Geodetic scientific complex. To detour to the summit tower, continue on the road uphill to the right. For our route, go left on the track beside the complex, which goes downhill slightly. (A sign here says no entry, so you should ask if there is anyone in sight. But the path/track skirts around the complex and does not enter it anyway.)

Follow this rough track down, in pleasant but quite remote forest, contouring around below the summit area. In about fifteen minutes you reach a junction. Take the right fork, going downhill in a series of turns. Soon you leave the forest and reach a village. At the water tap take the right hand track downhill. Keeping to the wide track, zigzag down around some houses to a schoolyard. Turn left here along the track, cross the yard ahead and follow the route as it twists and turns down the hillside to a large tree shrine with various rock lingams and two bells. This is about one hour from the top.

The track continues to drop around the hillside. Ignore a track on the right and contour round to a rocky stream and pool. The track now meets another wide track coming from the left, and heads right up a little to a forested saddle and spur. At the next junction, on top of the saddle, take the right fork downhill. Continuing through pleasant rural countryside, about three hours from Nagarkot, you reach a wider dirt road and Nala village.

Nala

If you are coming down from Nagarkot, you come to the Karunamaya complex to the northwest of Nala before the main village. The white deity, Karunamaya, is a version of one of the Buddhist Lokeshvaras and is closely related to Machhendranath. The image hides behind two security doors under an impressive torana. Two small stupas and a pond are in front of the temple. The Nala Lokeshvar Jatra is an annual spring festival that pays homage to Karunamaya and also to Dipanker, both Buddhist deities. The village is primarily a Hindu settlement, so this shrine could well pre-date the village.

In the centre of the village is a temple dedicated to Bhagawati. This unusual four-storied temple is particularly attractive; not many four-tiered temples are to be found in the valley. Four well-sculpted images adorn the temple struts. Five columns stand before the shrine, with lions and a peacock as guardians. On the south side are two attractive pitha resting-places.

Not far away to the southwest in one of the village's old streets is a superb stone sculpture, said to be Vishnu, with the deity sitting on a birdman figure. It is similar to the Mahavishnu image at Changu Narayan. A fine chaturmukha lingam also sits here. You may pass these two sculptures on your way from the Karunamaya to the Bhagawati temple.

Banepa

Some four kilometres southeast of Nala is the town of Banepa, just outside the valley, on the road to Tibet. At one time its territory extended along the Sun Kosi river. Situated on the trade route to Tibet, much of its wealth was generated by trading. Although at first appearance it is substantially modern, tucked away north of the road is the old village. In fact old Banepa is very clean and the newer buildings are not generally out of character.

If you are walking down from Nala, you will reach a junction before the main road. Old Banepa is to the left. Continuing on past a pond and brick stupa, there is a courtyard on the left containing two medium-sized **Vishnu Narayan** temples, each with two tiers and with a Garuda facing them. Further along the street is a Buddhist temple, with two beautifully sculpted stone Buddhas outside, as well as a four-faced chaitya with the Dhyani Buddhas.

Further on again, you come to a major junction with a large tank on the left. The water is a lurid green, but the overall impression is peaceful and attractive. At this junction a sign indicates that the **Chandeshwari** Temple is one kilometre away to the left. This temple is dedicated to Chandeshwari, a young and seductive manifestation of Durga, also known as Bhagawati. She is the daughter of Nara Devi / Sweta Kali in Kathmandu, and she reputedly rescued the townsfolk from the demon Chand.

Follow this road down and then up a short steep hill past the hospital. Soon you will see the imposing temple in the near distance, in a lovely forest setting by the river. Keep going until you reach a barrier beyond which no cars may pass. Continue on and through the brightly painted arch. Here you enter a large courtyard. Straight ahead is a small Shiva shikhara-style temple, with Nandi in attendance outside.

The main temple is three-tiered, with carvings on all levels and all struts, and an elaborate gajura. These carvings are said to represent the eight matrikas (Astha Matrikas) and eight Bhairabs. Facing the temple are five tall stone columns. Two of these are topped by peacocks, two by dragons, and one newer, smaller one by a tiger. The main torana is carved in wood. The temple is often closed, but even when open it is impossible to see the idol, as it seems to be hidden to one side. On the west side of the shrine is a brightly painted Bhairab.

If you go straight on through the courtyard, you can go down to the ghats on the Punyamati river, but it is not a particularly appealing prospect!

Walking back from the Chandeshwari temple, on the right is a low archway leading into a courtyard below a smaller three-tiered temple. This has an attractive wooden façade and torana.

Panauti

Panauti is close to Banepa, at the end of a pleasant valley dotted with traditional farmhouses set on hillocks above the fertile rice fields. A new Information Technology college and part of the Kathmandu University are also attractively-styled new buildings. Panauti is situated at the confluence of two rivers and a third mystical river, Saraswati. It has several interesting buildings and is well worth a visit if you are over here. The old part of Panauti has many fine four-storied Newari houses and is well kept.

The large main temple here is a Shiva temple, with one of the oldest lingams of the whole area. The temple is called **Indreshwari Mahadev Mandir**, and was constructed in 1294, before the Kasthamandap temple in Kathmandu. The 1988 earthquake partially destroyed this complex but it has now been beautifully restored. The temple is situated in the middle of a large courtyard; it has three tiers and all the struts are carved. A smaller two-tiered Shiva 'pagoda' stands next to the main temple.

On the south side is a **Bhairabnath** temple, with three figures facing outwards. On the east side are three sculpted stone images of Narayan, Lakshmi and Parvati. A large Narayan statue stands in the brick temple at the western gate. A small café is also near this gate.

There is a famous legend told in Panauti about **Ahilya**, the beautiful wife of a local wise man. The god Indra became passionately enamoured of Ahilya and, assuming human form, he seduced her. When the wise man heard of this, he put a curse on Indra, covering him with female yonis and making him live in seclusion by the two rivers in Panauti. Parvati, Shiva's consort, took pity on **Indrayani**, the consort of Indra, and relieved her of the suffering by making her into the third invisible river. Shiva later released Indra from the curse. There is a column devoted to Ahilya in Panauti.

There are two other temples in Panauti down by the river. On the south side is a complex dedicated to **Krishna**. Holy men often sit in meditation here amongst the jumble of shrines. Across the suspension bridge is the restored temple of **Brahmayani**, a rare manifestation of Brahma's consort.

Dhulikhel

Just four or five kilometres further east of Banepa is the hill town of Dhulikhel. Away from the main road and bus stops, the old village is quite attractive with only limited modernisation. On the west side of the village is the three-tiered **Bhagawati** temple with tiled lower walls. Each roof is gilded and birds decorate the corners. The crowning gajura is also an intricate balance of workmanship, with four nagas as part of the design. In the central part of old Dhulikhel are the **Vishnu** and **Harisiddhi** temples near a pond.

The old-time favourite place to stay, Dhulikhel Lodge, is now closed, but the original owners have now moved to a spectacular viewpoint north of the bus stop. The place is grander and is now called the Dhulikhel Lodge Resort.

Namo Buddha

Namo Buddha is well outside the valley, but of some significance. It is located near to the Himalayan resort town of Dhulikhel. It is about a three-hour walk from Dhulikhel. This sacred spot commemorates the actions of the **Buddha Shakyamuni**'s selfless actions to feed a starving tiger by offering his own flesh. The tiger was intent on catching a small boy for his supper. Stories such as this are found in the old Jataka tales, the folktales of the bodhisattvas, of which there are thousands. This place is one of the main pilgrimage sites for Tibetans.

The white-painted stupa here is more than twenty feet high and has the Tibetan-style bulging top part. It is topped by a mini Swayambhunath-style upper gilded tower with similar levels and is invariably covered with prayer flags. The toranas show the Dhyani Buddhas on the four cardinal sides. Various other houses and shrines are here, while close by is a monastery complex.

CHAPTER TEN
To the South of Kathmandu

Patan

In 1974 the Patan Durbar Square was not quite derelict but very rundown, with so much grass and weeds growing on the temple roofs that they were in danger of falling over. In the spring of 1975 work had already begun to restore these fine palaces. What we see today is a marvel to behold, with magnificent vistas of temples.

Patan is a city of artisans and remains a Buddhist town, despite recent influxes. At one time half the townsfolk were thought to have been monks, the rest being mostly artisans. Parts of it are very old. The Ashokan stupas are believed to be over 2400 years old. Patan was more important than Kathmandu in the Licchavi period. In the 7th century it was one of the major Buddhist centres of Asia. Patan flourished under the Malla Kings, but as Hindu ideas came into prominence it did not expand further. After the Shah Kings routed the valley, Kathmandu assumed the role of the leading city. Today Patan has expanded considerably and it is now effectively joined to Kathmandu. Patan is also known locally as Lalitpur (city of beauty).

There are four pleasant restaurants around Durbar Square. The Taleju at the south end has a high terrace with panoramic views. Also here is the Layaku Kitchen, a wonderfully restored place with a tremendous atmosphere. At the north end is another old house with a terrace, the Café du Temple, and in the northeast corner is another renovated café above a music shop, called the Old House Café. No modern buildings can be seen from here. No visit to Patan Durbar Square is complete without at least one evening visit. Invariably you will hear temple music and devotional chanting.

The boy of many languages, Patan 1975

As we came around the Patan Royal Palace a young boy approached, "Namaste, haben Sie ein Bic? Avez vous un bic? One pen you have sir," he said. Who was this grubby interloper? "You sir, English yes." We nodded with a "Yes" and a "Namaste". "I take you my house, very good view from there." We followed the boy for what seemed an age but was probably just a block away. The bazaar was very crowded and progress slow amid the cacophony of loud Nepali voices. Did you ever hear a Nepali speaking quietly?

The house had a low roof; inside it was very dark. A kerosene cooker gave out the mixed smells of cooking rice, garlic and the strong paraffin-like smell of unburned fuel. The boy led us up some steep narrow stairs. Another floor more and we stood on a flat area. It was the only flat roof in sight, this whole floor being an addition to the old house that seemed to be attached in a precarious fashion. "Dass ist wunderbar, ja? C'est tres joli, n'est-ce pas?" said the boy, forgetting momentarily that we were English. His French was better than mine, to be sure. We got versions in Italian and Spanish as well. This boy would go far and had obviously grasped the tourist message firmly. To make quick rupees in Nepal, you had to speak with the foreigners.

The view over the bazaar was great. We were easily parted from our rupees, but in a polite and impressive manner.

November Full Moon 2002

After some three hours of temple forays, we were in need of tea. The exquisitely restored Layaku Café was the place. Upstairs is a long Newari-style room with low tables and cushions facing out through the steeply-banked wooden windows overlooking the square. Red glazed bricks and wood characterise the construction materials. "Welcome, you are not fresh tourists, what are you doing here?" asked the charming manager. We explained and enjoyed our afternoon tea.

As the sun cast long shadows in the square, the atmosphere changed from quiet serenity into a more frenzied pace. Market stalls were set up, the ticket booth closed, tourists disappeared and the square came alive with glowing candles, light bulbs and floodlights that gave a mystical dreamlike quality to the temples. The trinkets departed and fresh fruit and vegetables took their place. People came to pay homage to their chosen deity. At the Krishna temple solemn chants rippled across the square; butter lamps twinkled as a full moon broke through the swirling dark clouds to reveal its shining white face.

The black silhouette of the Taleju temple stood stark and bold, as the moon traced its arc behind the second tier of the sacred shrine.

It was a magical, spellbinding moment.

Patan Durbar Square

The Patan Durbar Square is perhaps the most visually stunning of the three in the valley. It is more integrated, has a magnificent Royal Palace and retains the traditional look. It has no Rana buildings in it and is pleasing to the eye. We can begin here from the Mangal Bazaar road, after a drink and overview at one of the rooftop cafés, of course.

The Royal Palace is the main complex on the right. Although work began before his time, Siddhi Narasingha Malla was responsible for most of the construction of this palace and much of what we see today. Subsequent Malla Kings added to the whole Durbar Square complex.

Just in front of the first chowk stand three statues. These are of Hanuman, Garuda and Narasingha. The first quadrangle is the **Sundari**

Chowk, in which we find a sunken bath known as **Tulsi Hiti**, probably constructed in the mid 17th century. It has some amazingly elaborate designs, sculptures and motifs. It is octagonal in shape, in honour of the eight nagas, considered here as deities of rain. Vishnu and Lakshmi can be seen riding on the back of Garuda. Above this we see images of Bhairabs, the Matrika mother goddesses and the Nagas.

The next square is the **Mul Chowk**, the living area of the Malla families. Siddhi Narasingha Malla's son, Shrinivasa, placed the statues of the Hindu gods Ganga and Jamuna, here later in 1666. The chowk has two Taleju temples within its boundary; one is a three-tiered pagoda, the other is a four-tiered octagonal pagoda on the northeast side. There are many carved struts all around the square, supporting the roofs of the four-sided complex. There are two in particular of the elephant god, Ganesh. In the centre is an image of Taleju's sister Yantaju. There are no erotic carvings in this quadrangle, but fine workmanship all round.

In the next section is the **Degutale Mandir**, which is the tallest pagoda. It is also a Taleju temple. It has been partially destroyed a number of times, but is again restored. The Mallas had as their main deity the Degutaleju goddess. Behind the temple is **Nasal Chowk**. In front of the Degutale temple in Durbar Square is a column shrouded by a canopy of naga serpent cobras. On top is a delicate bird. One king, **Yoganendra Malla**, became a wandering sage after the death of his son. The statue was to be kept cleaned and the bird left untroubled until his return. They are still waiting.

The next quadrangle along is the **Mani Kashav Narayan Chowk**, also occasionally called the **Lumjyal Chowk**. This pleasant place is now a museum. The Museum is the fruits of many projects over years. Gotz Hagmuller has done the most recent work. He also worked on the Bhaktapur restoration project. Artefacts here are some of the most impressive Hindu, Buddhist and Tantric examples. The 12th century Uma Maheshwar sculpture has been sent back from Berlin.

The large open sunken bath just after the palace is called Mani Dhara or **Manga Hiti**, and is believed to be the oldest structure in the square. Lakshmi keeps watch here. Three waterspouts issue forth water. Another sunken bath was once also here, but has been covered over. The **Mani Mandapa** are the two open pavilions found here.

We are now at the far end of the square. The **Ganesh temple** at the north end between the two cafés has been recently renovated, and has a

Patan Durbar Square

Sketch Map of Patan Durbar Square

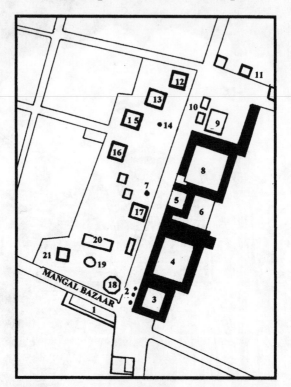

Key to Sketch Map of Patan Durbar Square

1 Café Layeku	11 Ganesh temple
2 Three statues	12 Bhimsen temple
3 Sundhari Chowk	13 Vishwanath Mandir
4 Mul Chowk	14 Garuda Pillar
5 Degataleju Temple	15 Krishna temple
6 Nasal Chowk	16 Char Narain temple
7 Yoganendra Malla pillar	17 Hari Shankar temple
8 Mani Kashav Narayan Chowk	18 Chyasin Dega temple
	19 Fountain
9 Manga Hiti	20 Shops
10 Mani Mandapa	21 Bai Dewala temple

colourful and lively statue of Ganesh dancing. On either side of him are two drummers. This manifestation is known as Nritya-Ganapathi, and his dance has a deep significance, comparable to Shiva's cosmic dance. With his left foot swinging, Ganesh makes the world appear and disappear. This dance reveals the heartbeat of the universe and its rhythm unites all manifestations. Turning around here, we can explore the western side of the square.

First we come to the **Bhimsen Mandir**, which is regarded as the temple of the merchants. Bhimsen is the god of merchants. It has some fine struts, carvings and bells as decoration. It is a Shiva-Bhairab shrine. Shrinivasa Malla built this temple. Note the metal strip hanging down the temple with a decoration at the base, this is a pataka, a guide for the gods to descend to earth. Musicians sometimes play temple music here in the evening.

Vishwanath Mandir, a Shiva temple is next. It was constructed around 1627. On the roof struts are images of Surya, the sun god, Ganesh, Annapurna, Shiva and Parvati amongst the collection. A Nandi bull guards the west of the temple and on the east are two large elephants.

The stone **Krishna Mandir** was built by Siddhi Narasingha Malla in 1637 and took over six years to finish. Its design is supposed to represent the mythical mountain Meru. There are some depictions of scenes from the Mahabharat, one of India's great epics. Garuda sits close by on a pillar facing the temple. Butter lamps flicker on the second level some evenings.

There are hardly any temples with erotic carvings to be found in Patan. The one that does exist is near the Indian-style stone Krishna temple. It is called **Char Narain** or Jagan Narayan, built sometime in the 15th or 16th century. It is devoted to Vishnu, the God of Preservation. This in itself may seem unusual, as most temples of erotic art seem to be devoted to Shiva. Vishnu is also found as Narain (also Narayan). This is one of the oldest temples in Patan and also has some of the more 'shocking' depictions.

The **Hari Shankar** temple is a large 17th century structure. The woodwork here is prolific, with six struts around the first level plus the corners and many more above. It has some interesting toranas. The shrine is unusual, in being dedicated to both Shiva and Vishnu. The **Bhai Dewal** temple is a Moghul-domed white shrine of little interest. A shop near here has the name of "Well Fit Tailors." Another large bell, similar to those found in Kathmandu and Bhaktapur, is seen hereabouts. Again it is a bell of the goddess Taleju, probably constructed in 1737.

The next Indian-looking temple is the **Chayasin Dewal**, an octagonal-shaped monument dedicated to Krishna. Krishna is the 8th avatar or incarnate of Vishnu, whose great love in life was Radha. This temple was constructed in 1723 under the tutelage of Yogmati, the daughter of Yoganendra Malla. She acted for a time as a regent, and by all accounts was an accomplished decisive ruler. Women rulers have been very rare in Nepal's history.

Bell

Patan Krishna Temple

Sketch Map of Patan

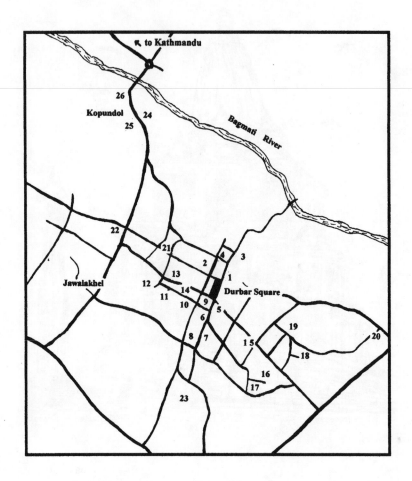

Key to Sketch Map of Patan

1	Vishnu temple	13	Bu Bahal
2	Kwa Bahal-Golden temple	14	Haka Bahal
3	Kumbeshwar Mahadev temple	15	Sundhara
		16	Mahabuddha temple
4	Bagalamukhi, Temple	17	Uku Bahal
5	Viswakarma Mandir	18	Bhimche Bahal
6	I Bahal Bahil	19	Su Bahal
7	Min Nath Mandir	20	Bal Kumari temple
8	Ta Bahal – Rato Machhendranath temple	21	Chandeswari temple
		22	Pulchowk Bahal
9	Hauga Bahal	23	Askok stupa
10	Asitanga Bhairab	24	Hotel Himalaya
11	Ajima temple	25	Pilgrims Book House
12	Punchali temple	26	Sikh temple

Temples to the North of Durbar Square

The original old city of Patan was to the north of Durbar Square. Heading north from the Bhimsen temple, we come first to a **Vishnu temple** with a Garuda in front and a parasol over him. This gives protection, joy and luck. It is the symbol of Vaikuntha, Vishnu in paradise. Vishnu is seen with four arms. Also around here is the **Uma Maheshwar** sculpture, a 10th century image of Shiva and Parvati on the right side.

Opposite here, down a small narrow lane beside a Krishna temple, is one of Patan's most interesting places. It is perhaps one of the most stunning visions in the whole valley. Here is the monastery complex of **Kwa Bahal**, which is its Newari name. It is now more commonly referred to as the **Golden Temple**, and was constructed around 1409. Kwa Bahal first appears to be mentioned in literature around 1081.The oldest artefacts in the complex date from 1398. Leather shoes should be removed in here, and a small entry fee paid.

The whole courtyard is a mass of intricate metal artwork. Many different smaller shrines ring the central edifice. The central smaller shrine is amazing, with images of Lokeshvara in different forms and the Dhyani Buddhas. Inside the temple is a silver stupa. On the west side is the three-tiered main temple, a stunning façade of gilded imagery. A long pataka hangs down and inside sits the serene Shakyamuni Buddha. Around the courtyard outer section are images of Vajrasattva, the priestly Buddha, the bodhisattvas, Padmapani and Manjushri, together with a beautiful Tara Buddhist goddess. The Dhyani Buddha, Amitabha is found here in his aspect of giving longevity and is called Aparmita, with his hands clasping a vase on his lap. A small monastery is located on an upper floor, with a white image of Avalokiteshvara. To the west side through a low passage is a large open square with a stupa and various chaityas.

We were lucky to have a magical evening visit to this wonderful temple, which is normally closed to the public at night. Inside the monks were chanting, and we were invited in to see them. The gold-plated temple is particularly stunning under the lights. Traditionally young boys are brought here to become monks for four days; once in January we saw this ceremony, when the young boys are naked and have holy water briefly poured over them, resulting in a quite a few tears in the cold weather!

Retracing our steps to the main street, we again continue north to **Kumbeshwar Mahadev**, a large complex of temples, tanks and shrines. The main temple is one of the oldest temples in Patan. Started in 1392, it originally had two tiers. Shrinivasa Malla added three more tiers in the 17th century. The temple is a Shiva temple, but here Shiva manifests as Khumbha, the lord of water vessels. Mythology implies that Shiva dwells here during winter to avoid the piercing cold at his usual residence, Mount Kailash. A large tank here is said to be linked to the Gosainkund Lake above Langtang, as are many other ponds around the valley. The Janai Purnima festival is celebrated here.

Opposite here is a shrine to **Bagalamukhi**, another form of the goddess Durga. She is the sender of diseases, usually cholera, in the monsoon period.

If you feel like a longer walk, then continue north from this area, following the road from Durbar Square past the northern stupa to **Jagat Narayan** on the banks of the Bagmati river. It was built in 1860 by Jagat Shumshere Rana. Here is a large complex with two main courtyards. The upper one houses the well-maintained brick shikhara-style temple of Jagat Narayan. Three very large images of Ganesh, Garuda and Hanuman are seen here, as well as an exquisite gilded Garuda high on a column. Various Hanuman images and a four-faced lingam dot the riverside ghats. This is a lovely place set in tranquil surroundings, well worth a detour.

A wide, solid motorbike and pedestrian bridge crosses the river and you can walk uphill from here to meet the road to Kathmandu near the Everest Hotel. Taxis collect here.

Temples to the South of Durbar Square

Heading almost south, the main street from Mangal Bazaar is full of fascinating shops and shrines. On the right is the recently restored (1995) **I Bahal Bahil** courtyard. Inside is a golden Buddha and some pilgrims rest places. This monastic building was first constructed in 1427 and represents a traditional monastery of Patan. Continuing south, we see on the left a large open sunken bath with three spouts.

Here we find the **Min Nath Mandir**, associated with Padmapani Lokeshvara, in a compound. Guarding the central shrine on both sides are lions, dragons and male figures. Prayer wheels, vajra and a stupa decorate the courtyard. A wooden torana sits above the main shrine; the goddess depicted has at least eight arms (and may be Mahalakshmi who stands on a lion). A small golden Buddha sits at its base. The main idol is Min Nath, a mini Machhendranath. He appears in the dark to be only about eighteen inches high and his little red face is only two inches or so across. His chariot follows the Red Machhendranath idol during the festivities. Across the street, down a small lane west, is home to one of the most famous idols of Patan and the valley in his red form.

One of the two homes of the Newari deity **Rato Machhendranath** is located here in **Ta Bahal**, a large partly grassy and mainly bricked compound. This is a magnificent temple and should not be missed. Machhendranath is also known as Padmapani, Bung Deo and Avalokiteshvara, depending on his colour. The Red Machhendranath idol is a strange-looking image with a very flat face and rather odd, unsettling eyes. He also has very large golden ears. He is the fish deity of plenty and rains. His festival is just before the monsoon.

On the main north side of the temple are some very well sculpted animals on low columns. These are a horse, elephant, peacock, Garuda, bull and a dragon. High on the temple are some exquisite carvings; some are erotic, others are rather horrific. On the east side a green snake is coiled around a hapless man. Other men are being boiled alive, while the demons stir the pots. A large stupa and a wide deep well are also here. The idol is normally enshrined here from autumn through till May.

In early May the Rato Machhendranath festival commences, and the idol is returned to Bungamati, five kilometres or so south of Patan, for the rest of the year.

Retracing your steps now back towards Durbar Square, you see a small lane on the left (west) side. This is an area of metalworkers and craftsmen. Down here are some hidden treasures. Almost immediately on the right is an unusual shrine, the temple of **Viswakarma,** the god of workers and their implements. This is one of Patan's best copper embossed gilded façades. Locals call it Vishnu Kamai or the **Hauga Bahal.** Across the narrow lane is a column on a tortoise and a modern building done well in the old style.

Further west is a Ganesh temple and then, as the alley widens, we find four small temples. At the south end is a mini three-tiered shrine to **Asitanga Bhairab**. Next to this is a Vishnu temple and two stone shikhara-style monuments. Continuing further west now, we reach a mini Ganesh temple. An Ajima goddess temple is slightly to the south down a narrow alley, just after an old tree that has grown across the alley at a height of about four feet. Again west from the Ganesh temple, we come to the **Punchali** temple near a small pond. This is a three-tiered gilded temple with, unusually, three gilded doors with three toranas above each door.

From here, turn right and right again at the main Mangal Bazaar road. On the way are some more bahals. The **Bu Bahal** on the north side has a large temple with tiled decorations, two lion/dragon figures with Buddha figures riding them, and various stupas. Shortly on the right is the **Haka Bahal**, home to the Kumari goddess of Patan. Her home was moved from Durbar Square to this building in the 17th century. Various lotus plinths, vajras, prayer wheels and oddities decorate the courtyard. The main shrine is impressive, with three serene Buddhas on the torana. The moon and sun gods are seen, as well as various lions. In the southwest corner is a marvellously-carved panelled area. Inside sits the sixth Dhyani Buddha, the Vajrasattva priest Buddha.

Heading southeast from Durbar Square through the bazaars, we come to **Sundhara**. Here is a large water tank with several spouts. The Red Machhendranath stops here for refreshments during his festival. Nearby is the **Mahabuddha** temple, a building influenced by the design of a temple in Bodhgaya in India. Pilgrims in the 17th century probably gave some ideas to the builders. It exhibits terracotta tiles, each having a Buddha on its surface. An amazing collection of bronze animals guards the temple of **Uku Bahal**, a monastic complex close by. The Uku Bahal dates from Licchavi times and is where the initiation rituals of the Kings took place. This practice was revived by Rudra Malla.

Return now to the main street that runs southeast from Mangal Bazaar. The southeast quarter of Patan still has many traditional streets.

Along the main street is a tree growing from a small shikhara temple and then, after two Ganesh temples, is a house on the right with some fine woodwork, including a peacock above the door. Ganesh, Kumar and Shiva are clear. This is a **Shiva-Parvati temple**. Heading vaguely north into the maze of old traditional streets, we find the **Bhimche Bahal**. It is a largish open area with a three-tiered temple. It has a stupa as its top gajura and a fine three-headed Buddha on the torana facing west. On one column are some inscriptions. Another mini-Swayambhu sits on a column. Nearby is the hidden **Su Bahal**, a courtyard within a courtyard. The images here are said to be Vajrasattva and Shakyamuni. In all at least six small Ganesh temples are found in this area.

A rather superb temple lies further out to the east from here. Set in relatively open country, in a large quadrangle, is the **Bal Kumari** temple. Four open stone chaityas sit at each corner of the courtyard. This three-tiered temple has latticed wood panels on the first level and some interesting figures. On the west side is an image of two dogs holding a decapitated human head! Erotic images are found here too. The top gajura is a multi-faceted version. The ground level of the temple is relatively open, with lions guarding the shrines. The main idol is flanked by Bhairab on the left and Ganesh on the right. The Kumari's vehicle, the peacock, sits high on a column. Some large kneeling 'donors' are on view here.

A number of other temples are dotted throughout the city. North of the main Mangal Bazaar road is the temple of **Chandeshwari.** This pleasant shrine has some fine woodcarving and sits at the northern side of a large tank or pond. A large stupa guards the western side of the pond, with four smaller stupas at each corner.

The famous grassy four **Ashokan Stupa** mounds are found at the four cardinal points of Patan; the western one is most easily visited. Not so long ago it sat on the very edge of the city. Behind the western stupa is the **Pulchowk**, Rateshwar Mahavihar (monastery) quadrangle. It has been recently remodelled, but houses one of the Ashokan-inscribed pillars. Some say a Vajra Yogini idol is found here.

Kirtipur

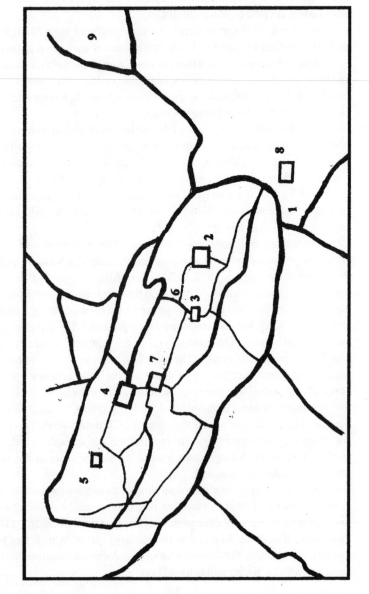

Sketch Map of Kirtipur

Key to Sketch Map of Kirtipur

1	Naya Bazaar	6	Chithu Baha
2	Chilamchu stupa	7	Narayan temple
3	Lohan Dega temple	8	Thai monastery
4	Bagh Bhairab temple	9	Tribhuvan University
5	Uma Maheshwar temple		

Kirtipur

Kirtipur was once an important town, guarding the entrance to the valley from India. Its ancient fort was considered impregnable, for Prithvi Narayan Shah tried three times to take it. In revenge he is said to have cut off the noses of all men over the age of twelve, except musicians. The old walls are only just visible, but the town boasts many water tanks and ponds. Today Kirtipur is starting to become modernised and its atmosphere is a little less traditional. But old corners can still be found here and there, with some particularly fine windows. Kirtipur was once the end of the cableway from Hetauda, near the Indian border town of Raxaul. Goods were ferried on this ropeway before the road was built, with loads taking three hours to reach the valley. There are four main structures here. Buses run between the Kirtipur Naya Bazaar and the Tundikhel/Ratna Park bus station.

Kirtipur in winter 1984

In 1984, Siân, her sister Kathryn and I cycled from Thamel to Kirtipur. The air was fresh, the valley resplendent, bathed in winter's dreamy light. From the Blue Star Hotel in Tripureshwar we crossed the Bagmati River to Patan. It was a hard cycle up the hill in Patan; the bicycles had no gears. From Patan we were into open fields and countryside, although the Tribhuvan University now occupied a lot of the land around Kirtipur. Climbing up here, the mountains sparkled on the northern horizon. Ganesh, Langtang,

> *Dorje Lhakpa, Phurbi Chyachu. Chobe Bamare, Gauri Shankar and the Rolwaling peaks as far as Numbur could be seen from west to east. Just below Kirtipur we spied the peak of Himalchuli visible half way towards Pokhara in the west, through the saddle of Nagarjun hill and the adjacent ridge.*
>
> *Kirtipur was pretty rundown and rather dirty, but the streets were full of local colour. People washing clothes, chickens picking at drying seed grains, dogs scowling and children, as always, rushing up to greet the strangers. A lot of Kirtipur seemed to be falling down. At the western end of town the forest seemed to be overtaking the place, monkeys leapt about causing consternation amongst the birds.*
>
> *Sleepy Kirtipur, what's happening there now?*

The **Chilamchu Stupa** is found on a hill in the south and is on a platform surrounded by four smaller stupas. Previously the bahal compound encircled the stupa. There is a very large vajra on the east side of the stupa. Heading west then north from here, we come to the **Lohan Deg**, a shikhara-style stone temple. Close by is the main temple of Kirtipur.

The **Bagh Bhairab** temple on the north side is a 16th century structure built to appease a tiger demon, according to one legend. This squat three-tiered temple has some good woodwork high up, with swords and shields attached that relate to the siege by the Shah King. It is impressive as a whole. Bhairab with ten arms is seen above the main door. An image of Hanuman on a column watches the temple courtyard. There are some goddesses stuck in concrete near the entry temple; these are mother goddesses and offer protection from evil spirits, diseases and famines. The view north is very impressive.

The **Uma Maheshwari** temple is located on the highest hill, guarded by two impressive elephants. This is a Shiva-Parvati temple. On the west side is an interesting image, probably the deity Mahalakshmi who has a sword, eight arms and is standing on a lion and a deer. Mahalakshmi is a form of Durga. The large bell here was made by 'Gillet and Johnston' in England in 1895.

Temple Door

Chobar Village and Gorge

The gorge and village of the same name are south of Kathmandu, and are famous as the place where the waters of the great Kathmandu Lake drained away. According to legend, the bodhisattva Manjushri slashed the earth with his sword to create the gorge. Images of Manjushri always have a large sword or knife as part of the image. Padma Sambhava, the Buddhist sage also known as Guru Rinpoche, is said to have meditated in the caves nearby.

The village is on a ridge near the gorge and can be accessed steeply from the northeast, less steeply from the south off the road to the Jal Vinayak temple, or up a small stone path from the Kirtipur side. On this route you pass a small Vishnu temple with some different idols. The main two-tiered shrine has a collection of tablets inside. In the yard are a four-faced lingam, a reclining image of Vishnu lying on snakes, a Garuda column and a large trident. If you come up the steps from the south side, you will arrive at a small shrine with two Garuda-like male and female figures (donors) looking at an image of the Dhyani Buddha, Amoghasiddhi, who always faces north.

One legend concerning Adinath Lokeshvara above Chobar is as follows. The bodhisattva was born of the essence of a jasmine flower to become the Adinath image above Chobar. One day during a festival in his name, his chariot got stuck in the river. Some say Adinath had at the time manifested himself as a beautiful maiden. Now Adinath the idol, or the maiden, was kidnapped during raids from the north and taken to Tibet. Assuming his bodhisattva image, he became known to the Tibetans as Phakpawati Chenresig and is still found at Kyirong, north of Langtang. Adinath used his divine powers to return to Chobar.

The main temple complex in the highest part of the village is devoted to **Adinath Lokeshvara** and dates from 1642. Lokeshvara has 108 images, of which Padmapani is a red-coloured one. For Hindus, Lokeshvara is Surya the sun god. Adinath is linked also to Karunamaya, Manjushri and Mahadev. The gilded three-tiered temple is adorned with an amazing number of pots and pans. Two lions, two kneeling figures known as the donors and a small stone shikhara temple watch over the main shrine. The image is very similar to the Red Machhendranath; it is red, its eyes give it a spaced-out look of resignation and it is adorned with a crown of nine serpents. An image of Padmapani Lokeshvara is on a mandala hanging from the ceiling above the red idol. This place is thought to have been in use since the Licchavi period. Couples come here to receive blessings for a good marriage, by offering pots and pans.

East of the main shrine is a small stupa and a small chaitya with a very colourful image of Krishna, his wife Radha, and a cow.

Jal Vinayak

The Jal Vinayak Mandir is an important temple devoted to Ganesh, located next to the river southeast of the Chobar Gorge. Built in 1602, it is a three-tiered temple with the first tier unusually high off the ground. It has some erotic art as well as the eight Bhairabs, the eight Matrikas and eight Ganesh images in different colours high up. Bells and lions guard the south-facing shrine. Ganesh himself is abstract, a large stone covered by a metal sheet. His image has a large gilded necklace and is topped by an archway of many bells. A large gilded rat crowns a column here, for the rat is the vehicle of Ganesh. People paying homage to Ganesh bring sweets and sour radishes to offer him for prosperity and wisdom. Around the shrine are arched, whitewashed pilgrims' quarters. The cement factory nearby is now defunct. The Taudaha pond further south along the road is a deep pool in which the snake serpent Kartotak now lives, surrounded by treasures, watching over the valley. Kartotak once lived in the great lake that was drained by the sword of Manjushri.

Dakshinkali

This is one of the most important shrines to the goddess Kali and is south of Kathmandu; dakshin means south. Bloody sacrificial offerings are made here, mostly on Saturdays and Tuesdays. Male animals are taken for ritual beheading and the blood is sprayed on to the idol. The image is macabre, black, with Kali holding a skull, a head and a sword. After the sacrifices, the dead animals are eaten for picnics. Kali is appeased and all is well; even the animals are believed to have gone to a better world. Images of Ganesh and Bhairab are also found nearby.

To reach Dakshinkali by local bus from Kathmandu city bus depot will take one hour or more (15 rupees one way). A taxi may cost 700 to 1000 rupees, depending on the time of your visit. A very pleasant and clean resort is found between Pharping and Dakshinkali; the Dakshinkali Village Inn ($15-25 first price). It has a great view of the Himalayas east from Langtang to Numbur. Traditional farmhouses are very close to the gardens. The restaurant is excellent for day-trippers, and it would be a wonderful place to spend the night. Hattiban Resort is another more expensive option.

Dakshinkali is just down a steep hill from here. The temple is located in a dense, shady forest, and is a favourite picnic spot on a Saturday when the main sacrifices take place. From the bus park follow the small tarmac road to its end, passing the garland and food sellers. There are picnic areas down steps to the left. Follow the one way in and out system across the river, where a newish dam provides washing pools. The two streams meet at the shrine. Sadhus often sit here.

Be sure to note the sign 'Visit our religious web site www.dakshinkali.org.' The main tiled courtyard sits below the four gilded nagas who support the canopy. Eight protecting dragon-like figures mark the entrance. Non-Hindus must watch from here. On the left amongst the idols are Buddha, Ganesh and the boar god, Varaha. The main idol of Kali is quite small, but garlanded with ornaments, marigolds and a gold crown. The goddess is black with white or gilded eyes that are not always visible. A resting-place here by the entrance depicts the goddess's different poses in a photographic display. On Saturdays many people come to offer chickens and goats for blood sacrifice to the goddess Kali. It is not for those of a sensitive disposition, but is fairly joyous for the local devotees. But on other days of the week it is a peaceful place, and the beautiful forest adds to the atmosphere.

Returning to the parking area, you can walk up to the Dakshinkali Village Inn for tea, or continue back to Pharping, which is half-traditional and half-modernised these days. It still gives a flavour of a large country village though.

Pharping

This village lies some 18 kilometres south of Kathmandu. From the Pharping 'football field' corner, follow the dirt road to the right (west) towards several monasteries. Turn right at the first one, up a small lane, then go left and come above the new monastery and impressive Tibetan-style Stupa, 40 feet high with a bulging dome. Continue along until you reach some steps up. Here are two monastery buildings. If you need a guide, ask for Kumar.

The Ganesh and Saraswati or **Twenty-One Taras Monastery** (Gompa) is on the left. In this context Saraswati is the Tara, connecting the Tibetan deities with the Hindu. Ganesh is in the rock, having appeared there naturally without human sculpting, and sits below the twenty-one Taras. They are encased in glass-fronted boxes around a larger main Tara. Local folklore says that three Taras have evolved from the rock and that eventually all twenty-one will appear in rock form. On the right is the Rigzin Phrodang Gompa. The main idol is Guru Rinpoche. An amazing blue, ferocious Chenresig (Avalokiteshvara) in yab-yum with his dakini sits to the right of Guru Rinpoche. They are decorated with garlands of heads and blue skulls. Her toenails are as vicious-looking as his teeth on each of his three heads. On the left is Dorje Soli? Between the two monasteries is a lingam, bringing Shiva into the scene.

Continue up the steep steps, passing the lingam and two waterspouts. Shortly on the left is a path that leads up to an open gully and an overhang. Here is the place where **Padma Sambhava** first meditated. Locals will point out his rock image and his footprint. An idol is seated here with butter lamps. Retracing your steps, continue up the main path, newly built.

After a few bends you reach the **Asura Cave** complex, said to be Padma Sambhava's main meditation cave. Here are two further small monastery buildings and the main monastery.

In the southern room are the Taras again. In the north is again Guru Rinpoche (Padma Sambhava). Between the two is a plinth of lotus and Vishnu's footprints. The main cave is quite small, black with smoke, and inside above the butter lamps is a black stone image of Guru Rinpoche. Each side of him are two visions of **Vajrakila**, one in yab-yum, representing the sharp focus of wisdom. Vajrakila is a tantric deity, who when seen in physical form, has a strange and awesome appearance. This is supposedly to focus one's attention and clear obstacles away, for those seeking enlightenment.

If you now continue down through the building, you will exit to the north and can walk the short distance down the hill to **Vajra Yogini**, a Tantric temple in a separate complex, the **Phampi Bahal**. This Vajra Yogini is occasionally known as the Indra Yogini, 'she who defeats all' and also as Nil Tara, the blue Tara. The temple is relatively recently painted and is modernised with marble and tiles. The three-tiered shrine sits on the back wall of the compound facing east. It has a golden pataka and an elaborate gajura.

Vajra Yogini is normally a fearsome aspect of the female Buddha and there are three other shrines in the valley devoted to her. This is one of her less ferocious forms. The Vajra is the thunderbolt or in Tibetan, the Dorjee. The goddess is the consort of Heruka. When in yab-yum position they are the subjects of the Heruka Tantras. Heruka is a terrible form of the Akshobhya Buddha.

On the ground level is the red idol of Vajra Yogini, with Shakyamuni Buddha on the right and, we think, Dorje Sambhava on the left. On the first roof level you can see two Surya sun gods at each end. Images of Padmapani Lokeshvara, Prajnaparmita and Vajrasattva are said to have been here too!

At certain times of the day you may be permitted to go upstairs to the next level. On the gilded torana above the main shrine, Vajra Yogini is in classic pose, looking to her left and holding her left leg up behind her shoulder. She is flanked by her Yoginis, Singhini (lion) and Baghini (tiger). Her Tibetan name is Dorje Nanjirma.

Sketch Map of Dakshinkali and Pharping area

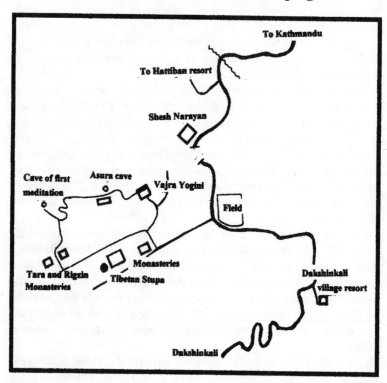

On the north of this floor is a door that leads to the Tibetan version of the deity. The other deity here is Dorje Forna, who is carried to the village of Pharping during a once-yearly celebration, leaving this abode by passing down through the trapdoor here.

You can now depart through the gates and go down the steep steps to meet the path you first came up from Pharping village. Further to the north on the hill is another Tibetan monastery in a beautiful forested setting. It has a red Lakhang (chapel) and white lower walls. Back at the corner, head north for five minutes to find the Shesh Narayan temple area.

Shesh Narayan

Shesh Narayan sometimes called Sheku or Shekha Narayan, is one of the four main temples to Narayan in the valley. It has a number of quiet pools decorating its approaches. On the left are two figures in the open area. Here are Garuda and Hanuman facing a building housing Krishna, seen in stone sculpture. On the other building are some erotic figures, which is unusual on Vishnu shrines A large lingam is also here in its own building. As you approach the steps, note the three lingams on the right, each with four faces in Chaturmukha format.

Up the steps, set below the yellow/white and brown streaked limestone cliff, is the single storey Shesh Narayan temple. The idol has been removed from the torana above the door. Garuda and Hanuman again watch over the temple. Inside Vishnu is standing with two arms up and two down. There is a Shiva lingam on this terrace. Just to the right is an image of Vamana, the dwarf version of Vishnu, and a **small low cave** where Padma Sambhava also meditated. The other building is said to house images of Balaram (Krishna's brother), the Green Tara, Padma Sambhava/ Guru Rinpoche and a bodhisattva.

Above the temple are very realistic **rock nagas**. Legend says that these represent the nagas who disturbed Padma Sambhava when in meditation. He struck one with his Vajrakila dagger and it now weeps at auspicious times. The Vajrakila is a symbol of concentrated wisdom focused as a sharp pointed object. Vajrakila can also appear in deity form, as a strange-looking idol, designed to clear away obstructions to enlightenment. It appears with three heads, six arms and four legs. It also has earrings of live snakes, amongst other strange adornments, including the more familiar trident.

A festival occurs here in mid-November, called Thulo (big) Ekadasi.

Shesh Narayan Temple, Pharping

Also to the right of the temple is a **Tibetan monastery** with Guru Rinpoche. This monastery is quite active. We were privileged to witness some meditation and prayer.

Below the monastery on the road north is another courtyard. Here we find Ganesh and Kumar each side of a lingam. Kumar has ten arms in warrior mode. Bhairab sits on the southern outer wall of the inner sanctum, sitting on heads and wearing a garland of skulls. Also in the outer courtyard we find Garuda, Nandi and a trident. Just up the road north is a chautara, a resting place below a pipal tree bedecked with hundreds of prayer flags.

On any day other than Saturday it is a pleasant walk along the road north towards Kathmandu. After passing the track to the Hattiban Resort, the road then passes through traditional rural scenes with terraces and farmhouses. Around the spur are views over the Bagmati, with Chapagaon in the distance to the east. Later you can see Bungamati and Khokana.

Bungamati

This lovely village is about 10 kilometres south of Kathmandu. It has retained a very pleasant atmosphere and is still almost completely untouched by new development. This has become a rare thing in the valley, apart from Bhaktapur. Life goes on much as it has for centuries; people draw water from wells, dry corn, rice and millet, children scurry everywhere. Men watch women do all the work. Bungamati became important during the reign of King Narendradeva when Bungadya, the most ancient and revered version of Lokeshvara in the valley, became known as Karunamaya Avalokiteshvara.

One legend recounts that Gorakhnath, a disciple of Machhendranath, came to the valley and being angered there, sat on the place where the nagas resided. The nagas became angry and they stopped the rains. In order to stop the droughts, messengers were dispatched to Assam to bring Machhendranath in order to resolve the situation. On the way great demons barred the way, but four Bhairabs cleared the route. Some legends say Machhendranath came in the disguise of a bee. When Gorakhnath saw his master Machhendranath, he ran to him and the nagas were released. The rains came and subsequently Machhendranath was worshipped in the valley.

Bungamati is the winter home of the Red Machhendranath. Bungamati is said to be where the Machhendranath first landed and became a deity of rainmaking in the valley. Most people will come from the main road and enter the square from the south, but the main entry is on the north side. Here is an arch and two lions. As you enter the square, there is a column sitting on a tortoise. On the top sits a serene Buddha with his vajra in his right hand at chest level. A bell is in his left hand on his lap. This rare idol is the sixth Dhyani Buddha, who acts as priest to the five main ones. He is called Vajrasattva. He never appears on chaityas or stupas and is worshipped in secret.

Sketch Map of Bungamati

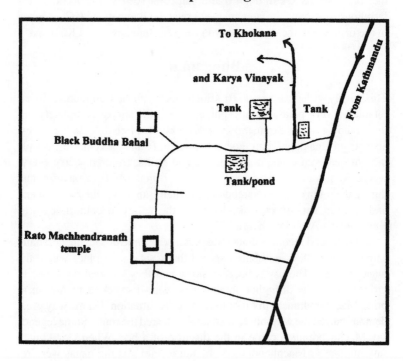

Bungamati: entry to Rato Machhendranath Temple square

The Red Machhendranath idol, if in residence, is found facing north in the central temple within the Bunga Bahal, which is ideal for drying corn and millet. The mainly white stone temple is one of the rare Buddhist shikhara shrines. Two lions guard the entrance. Three bells are also seen on the north side. On each of the lower four main walls of the temple are two stone Buddhas with hands in different positions on each wall. Toranas above the other doors show forms of Manjushri. A priest from Bungamati attends the idol even when it goes to Patan. There are various other shrines around the main structure. One contains a black Bhairab. Another has the Buddha images. In the southeast corner is a two-tiered Bhairab temple, but it is usually locked.

If you now continue north from Red Machhendranath down the steps and along the lane, you come to a corner, and off to the left here is a hidden gem. Across the courtyard, past two chaityas with Dhyani Buddhas, is an enclosed **bahal**. You may have to ask someone to let you in. If you are lucky you enter the building and come face to face with an unusual temple, which has an open wooden-structured top tier. On the right is an inscription plate. Gilded banners, bells and lions appear here, as well as an unusual lingam sitting in a square yoni. Some worn frescoes are also found in the courtyard, including a line of Rajasthani-like people sitting in a long boat. The idol in the two-tiered temple is a serene black Buddha-like figure. No one knew its name.

Walk from Bungamati by taking a path north on the west side of a pond on the way out from the above area. In about fifteen minutes, at a school, the path divides. The left track goes to a small Ganesh temple up some steps. This is called **Karya Vinayak**. The panoramic view from here is excellent. Ganesh is abstract, but has seven nagas above his image. His rat vehicle sits on a low column. The sun and moon gods peep out here. It is as usual a popular place of worship. The right hand path leads to Khokana.

Khokana

Another unspoilt Newari village, another magical place to step back in time. You can take a circular tour by heading left from the entry tank area. Again everyday life continues down here. Turn down to the right and shortly you come to the main temple that foreigners cannot enter. The three-tiered temple is devoted to **Shekali Mai**, a goddess sometimes known as Rudrayani. (Shiva was first known as Rudra and his consort was then

Rudrayani). By continuing down and making two further right turns you can make a complete circuit of this charming country village. Oil-making is a traditional activity in this village and the old oil presses have recently been restored.

From Khokana it is possible to do a very enjoyable trek to Pharping and Dakshinkali. Take the path down south-west towards the river, cross the river on a substantial suspension bridge, then go straight ahead up the steps until you reach the wall surrounding the leprosy clinic. Turn right, then left to reach a dirt road. Take the path opposite steeply uphill until you reach the main tarmac road. From here you can take a public bus, or whatever comes along, to Dakshinkali. (Note that you must take care to find the correct path out of Khokana as there is a plank bridge further north.)

Chapagaon

On a different road to the south of Patan is Chapagaon, another small Newari village. The main attraction of Chapagaon is the shrine of **Vajra Varahi**, which is in fact in the forest just outside the village on the east side. Many people picnic in the forest after their sacrifices. Hanuman greets you as you arrive at the temple, shaded by a parasol, and there will often be a band playing music. Facing the temple, looking east, is a large Nandi bull. Worshippers climb up the adjacent steps to pour milk and red vermilion powder over him. Various lingams are found in the courtyard; one is a splendid four-faced black example. Lions guard the central, two-tiered temple. Latticed panels enclose the sides of both levels and there is no gajura on the top. Four impressive patakas hang down.

Above the main west-facing entrance are three toranas. On the central one is the main deity, Vajra Varahi, the boar-headed goddess with eight arms; she is flanked by three figures on each side. Inside the temple, a snake arch tops the visions of the goddess and two demonic companions. Devotees enter from the south, with animal sacrifices. Tuesdays and Saturdays are the main days of devotion; definitely not for the squeamish. People ask for good fortune for their livestock.

A new Buddhist monastery to the south offers a less lurid sanctuary.

Chapagaon village itself is now a bit rundown. Some parts are still traditional, but rather dirty in places. In the main street are two smallish temples. The larger **Bhairab** temple has some interesting erotic images on the first level; one on the east side involves three people! The toranas are in wood. Two ugly protectors are swallowing images. A birdman protector sits at the top. The smaller temple is devoted to Vishnu. Along the main street to the south is a very old single-storied temple. It has a simple embossed torana and a Bhairab, three-eyed mural inside.

Thecho

The village of Thecho is more pleasant aesthetically, having more old traditional streets and a few newer houses. A street leads west from the main tank in town to the **Bal Kumari** temple. A peacock column faces the main shrine, which is a three-tiered structure. On the second level pots and pans adorn the front face. Ganesh helps to bring prosperity on the right of the closed entrance. In Thecho is one of the rare temples devoted to the goddess Brahmayani. The temple is to the northern end of the village, and again on the west side of the road. Again very unusual is the goddess's vehicle, the goose, on a high column. The temple is also rectangular with two lattice-panelled tiers and a simple gilded window. A stupa sits on the south side. There are said to be some old oil presses around Thecho.

Sunakothi

This place is a small settlement straddling the road to Chapagaon. It has a complex devoted to Shiva on the east side of the road. A massive bull and stone trident dominate the courtyard. An equally massive lingam is found inside the temple, which has a domed stupalike roof. On the southwest corner is probably the smallest two-tiered mini pagoda shrine in the valley, complete with gajura. Another whitewashed mini-temple sits outside the courtyard on the east wall, with Ganesh and a large stone stupa-topped chaitya with Dhyani Buddhas in residence.

Lele

Lele is on the southern edge of the valley. In the hills here is the **Tika Bhairab**. This mural-like shrine shows the three-eyed Bhairab sitting in the ground. He has two large eyes with one above. He is said to be one of the four Bhairabs who helped to escort Machhendranath from Assam to the Kathmandu Valley and who helped protect him against angry demons.

Blood sacrifices are performed throughout the year. The image is painted just once a year.

Harisiddhi

Harisiddhi is located southeast of Kathmandu, on the way to Godavari. The four-tiered Tantric temple here is devoted to another aspect of Durga, that of **Harisiddhi Bhavani**. Harisiddhi was a goddess who was brought here from India. There is a dance festival held in honour of the Goddess Harisiddhi. In ancient times every twelve years, human sacrifices, which are now outlawed, took place. Archaeologists have suggested that Harisiddhi might have been much bigger. Traces of a sunken temple have been found nearby, buried in the nearby fields and only located by the remains of two lions. Otherwise it's a sleepy rural place with dogs, and notably a dance troupe who perform here occasionally.

Godavari

Godavari is an open place with a few buildings at the foot of Pulchowki Hill. Here is the botanical garden, with orchids in particular, but also many other Himalayan plants on view. Rhododendrons adorn the Pulchowki Hill, the place of flowers, in spring. Hindu pilgrims gather at the sacred spring here every twelve years in a mela (gathering). Pulchowki Mai is the mother goddess of the forest and a shrine exists here in her honour.

Lubhu

Lubhu is located southeast of Patan along a rough road which passes many brick-making facilities with their small chimneys. The village still retains a rural feel, with grain scattered across the road during harvest times, but quite a lot of new building is evident.

The main three-tiered temple sits in a courtyard and is devoted to **Mahalakshmi**, an aspect of Bhairavi, the female consort of Bhairab. This temple is worshipped for prosperity but is itself devoid of many idols or decoration. It did have some gaily-painted resident tortoises though when we visited.

The ruins of a fort are said to exist here, but exactly where is unclear. On the south side of the village is a rather rundown Shiva complex. Other smaller shrines, Ganesh, Krishna and Vishnu etc are dotted throughout the village. Of more interest are the many family-run weaving mills found throughout the village, in often dark and small old houses.

CHAPTER ELEVEN
To the West of Kathmandu

Balaju

Now a suburb of Kathmandu, just outside the ring road, it is noted for its water gardens and the smaller **sleeping Vishnu** here, as well as some small temples. At one time the water gardens were very elaborate and in a quiet, almost country, setting.

Not far away, but actually within the ring road, is a very well hidden temple located on a very steep little bamboo-clad hill. This is the temple of **Mahaipi** or Mahidevi. Mahaipi is one of the Astha Matrika, Mother Goddesses, a protector against diseases. This shrine can be reached by following the east bank of the Vishnumati River from the bridge of the road coming from Thamel. There are about 160 steep steps up to the main temple area. As you begin you will see some Buddha feet on the ground.

The main temple is a glazed brick two-tier structure with a small abstract rock idol deep inside. Set below a golden altar, the idol has a golden crown and is covered in food and flower offerings. Around the inside of the temple are several stone images, including a Nandi bull. Around the entrance door are 13 stone images, and Ganesh greets the devotees on the southern side. New struts indicate some renovation here. Also in the courtyard is Krishna and a Shakti Narayan, a Tantric consort of Vishnu. A small monastery sits next to the main temple with a central Shakyamuni Buddha and a medicine Buddha in the right corner.

There is also said to be a **Sikh** temple, easily overlooked; so easily overlooked that we missed it too! It is said to contain a holy book possibly written by Guru Nanak, founder of the Sikh religion.

Nagarjun Hill

This is said in myth to be the place from where the lotus seed was thrown into the lake that was once in the valley. It is where the Indian sage Nagarjuna meditated in a cave on the hill. Others believe a mythical sage threw the lotus seed into the lake that grew to become Swayambhu. During the Lhuti Punhi festival, Buddhists climb to the summit, called Jamacho, in reverence for their dead ancestors.

The Ranas used the hill for hunting deer, wild boar and even leopard. It is now a Royal Reserve and can be climbed from the main gate, on the road from Balaju towards Dhunche/Langtang. The trek is a wonderful escape from the pollution of the city itself, and a good chance to experience trekking in Nepal if you don't have the time or inclination to go on a longer trek. The climb up takes about two hours; take food and water, and allow just over an hour for the trek back down. There is a Buddhist stupa and temple at the top, and an exciting viewing tower. A dirt road also runs up to the summit, but this is considerably longer and not suitable for walking.

> ## *Nagarjun — a walk up in December 2001*
>
> *Just outside the Kathmandu ring road lies a hidden paradise - the forest of Nagarjun. Beyond the city, yet only twenty minutes or so by taxi, lies the entrance gate to the Royal Forest (the entry fee was Rs. 10 each in Dec. 2001), on the road to Dhunche and Langtang, up past Balaju. From here you climb almost instantly into a forgotten land of birds and greenery, a lost world. The initial part of the trail is steep and uncompromising, but it soon becomes more gentle and even level in a few places! Wandering serenely through the trees, the hustle and bustle of Kathmandu metropolitan city seems a world away.*
>
> *In the distance, through gaps in the dense forest, the white peaks of the Himalayas will show themselves if the weather is clear; from Numbur (towards Everest) in the east to Langtang, Ganesh, Himalchuli and even*

the Annapurnas, seventy miles away to the west. To the south are the hills surrounding the Kathmandu Valley. This truly is the top of the world, and so close to the city. You don't need to go trekking to get stupendous views! After two hours the summit is reached, and another surprise lies in store — a Buddhist stupa, small temple and a large Buddha statue.

There seem to be a thousand prayer flags fluttering in the cool fresh breeze, and the views all around from the tower are quite out of this world. Simply breathtaking, especially at the altitude of 7000 ft!

One hour and ten minutes should suffice for the descent, but take great care, the path is slippery in places. And don't forget to take your own food and drink, as there are no refreshment stalls along the way.

Sadly then, the dream is over, reality hits you as you return to the road, but paradise can't last forever ... or can it?

A Trek to Machha Narayan

This half-day trek takes in pleasant country lanes, farming landscapes, Himalayan views and some little-visited temples. Our walk begins just outside the ring road, heading out on the Thankot road from Kalanki junction. About one and a half kilometres from the junction is a small road off to the left, which opens out with views of the western end of Kirtipur. A taxi from Thamel to the end of the tarmac might be Rs. 350-400.

From here you follow the rough stony road downhill to a collection of small shrines by a stream, off to the right. The main shrine, next to the large tree, has a small golden image of **Vishnu Devi**. All about are various small images and deities.

Continuing on now, the main track drops down into fields and then begins a steady climb to the village of **Toukhel**. A quick look around here reveals some well carved stone Dhyani Buddha chaityas and some traditional Newari houses. People seem glad to see some visitors; the dogs may not be so happy! Follow the road around the village and after a short descent again climb steadily up to the village of Machhegaon, where we find the shrine of Machha Narayan. Allow up to one hour's walk.

Machha Narayan

Sitting just below the south-western rim of the valley in a lush grove is the isolated shrine of **Maccha Narayan**, in the village of **Machhegaon**. There are three main temples in the village, which is very rural and quiet. Coming uphill from the entrance arch, you find the cool pool of the Machha Narayan temple. The small white temple with a dome-like top is the main shrine. It is open from 6 am to 9 am in the mornings, when the fish-faced image of Vishnu is visible in the gloomy chamber. The fish is the first avatar of Vishnu. Outside is a Garuda guarding the shrine, with Hanuman to the right. Large orange fish swim in the pool and trees shade the whole area. A festival takes place here every three years.

Across the street is a large bathing and washing tank with water-spouts. Uphill again is the **Vishnu Devi** three-tiered whitewashed temple with two stone lions at the entrance. It has terracotta tiled roofs and the main deities are hidden upstairs. The young boys here were very helpful and informative, inviting us inside to view the deities. Here we saw Ganesh, Kumari, Vishnu, Kalika and Bhairab; five golden faces covered in flowers, vermilion and food offerings. In the window is another deity known by the locals as 'Kal Bhairab'.

Further through the village is an unusual modern image of a **reclining Buddha**.

A Trek to Balambu

Returning through the village to the entrance arch, look for a dirt road up to the left and follow this road out of the village. After passing the Jyoti Academy and a bamboo clump, you come to agricultural land. Soon the road passes under the old cable ropeway, which was the only means of getting goods up over the mountains from India before any roads were built in Nepal. Not far from here you reach the new Korean-built Khushi Khushi resort, where there is a good restaurant with a great view to Swayambhu, Kirtipur and the Himalayas beyond. It was a great relief to find this on a hot sweaty June day!

From here you can walk on to reach a new tarmac road in about 10 minutes. The walk down to the main road is about half an hour, or less if a bus comes by. You reach the main road at Satungal, another old Newari village which is rapidly modernising. There is a shrine here, again devoted to Vishnu Devi. Across the road is a small but well-kept shrine housing a voluptuous goddess under a canopy of five snakes, flanked by Ganesh and Kumar. From here you can return to Kathmandu, or continue to Balambu, which is about 10 minutes along the road towards Thankot.

Balambu

To visit Balambu, turn right off the main road where you see a beautiful chaitya of **Dhyani Buddhas**. This village has retained many old houses and is a traffic-free zone. After the black **Shakyamuni Buddha** figure is a small three-tiered whitewashed temple, guarded by two stone lions. This is the shrine of **Mahalakshmi**. It has no torana, but it has a stone arch over the door with eleven stone carved images. Wooden toranas are, however, seen on the two building adjacent to the main temple.

Along the street on the right is a new but well-made copper image of **Ganesh**. Continuing down through the village, you see a fine chaitya and then a **small white stupa** with eight Buddha images on it. Downhill you leave the village and cross the river by another Ganesh shrine. From here you can return the same way to the main road, or continue on through very pleasant farming country to the metropolis of Kathmandu.

A Trek from Balambu to Kathmandu

From the river follow the track to a junction. Take the right path towards a brick factory, which you might be able to visit. Continue past the factory on a narrow path just left of the guardhouse. This path crosses open countryside of rice terraces with traditional farmhouses on the ridge to the north. Eventually the path widens and you climb up to the village of Naikap topped by a couple of shrines.

From here various roads go down to the east. We took a road just left of the top shrine, which came to a junction soon. Going left, we contoured around to a tree and then we cut down past some small houses on a footpath until we met a rough road. We went right here and continued on down, passing some modern houses and into the jumble of suburbs. There are a few old houses here.

When you come to a T-junction, go right to meet the main road at Kalanki. Go left to the main ring road junction and look for transport into town.

Thankot

This small village on the western edge of the valley has been largely destroyed in the rush for modernisation, and also because its narrow streets were too small to accommodate the increased traffic from India. The Chandragiri pass not far away marks the western rim of the valley. It has a temple located out of town, dedicated to **Bhagawati**.

Ichangu Narayan

This is located to the west of Swayambhunath, below a spur of the Nagarjun hill. It is one of the main Vishnu Narayan sites in the valley, but is not on the same scale as Changu Narayan near Bhaktapur. The walk out is quite pleasant, once you leave the chaos of the ring road. The rough road climbs to the village of **Halchak**, with a small shrine, and then continues through very attractive countryside. It may be possible to persuade a taxi driver to take you there and back for around Rs. 200.

The temple itself sits in a fairly empty courtyard, but is shaded by trees on the western end. A stone plinth greets you on arrival, with images of **Narayan** and **Hanuman**. In the far corner is a separate quadrangle with a small shrine to **Mahalakshmi**.

The main temple has two tiers, but in addition there is unusually a separate tier over the entrance to the shrine. The main idol is Narayan, holding some of his symbols in four hands. At the entrance we see two short columns, topped with Vishnu's symbols the chakra and conch shell. Both pillars sit on squashed stone turtles. Colourful birdman figures crown the first level and some simple carvings decorate the upper level.

Swayambhunath

Far from the madding crowd, or perhaps not anymore, to the west of the city is the hill of Swayambhunath, also known as the **Monkey Temple** because of the large number of monkeys that live there. Swayambhu means 'the self-created.' It is said to be the divine lotus flower floating above the lake that once covered the Kathmandu Valley. This is the most famous image of all Nepal; the all-seeing stupa gilded with gold, its eyes surveying every corner of the valley.swayambhu is worshipped as the Adi Buddha, the Buddha without beginning or end. The Adi Buddha is primordial and the eyes are his. The Adi Buddha as Vajradhara is often seen in the tantric yab-yum position with his dakini, a tantric demon goddess. He also reveals himself as a blue flame emanating from a lotus. Padma Sambhava, the tantric 'magician' is believed to have come here.

If you climb up the steps from the Kathmandu side, be careful not to stop and eat a banana—you may get an unwelcome visit from the monkeys, which are potential rabies carriers and should be treated with caution. On every corner of the temple they sit, leaping vigorously and spontaneously from one spot to another, sometimes screeching at each other as they race around the monuments.

Near the top of the innumerable steps is the entry post where you will be asked to pay your admission fee. After this you will certainly need to catch your breath for a few minutes; though the fee is not high, the steps are! Just in front of the stupa here on the east side, you find a strange-looking golden object called a **dorjee**, placed on a stand surrounded by various colourful animal forms including a cow, a golden lion, a sheep and the nine others representing the twelve Tibetan signs of the zodiac. This dorjee, also called a vajra, is a tantric symbol, the thunderbolt, the destructive aspect of the God Indra. In Tantra the dorjee is the male principle, the bell is the female. On either side of the dorjee is a huge bell, which will be rung by devotees as they circumnavigate the stupa. And beyond these bells, again, one on each side is a tall white Indian-style temple.

Walk round the stupa **clockwise**, as you should always do with any Buddhist stupa, chorten or other monument. To the left the view across the valley is outstanding; the development over the last few years will stagger anyone who is returning after some time away, as from here you can see most of the valley. On the south side is the **Vasupur** shrine dedicated to Vasundhara, the earth goddess, and the marble **Vayupur** shrine. Also here are many small chaityas, and a white five-stepped stupa with many small Buddhas and other figures carved into niches in its sides.

Opposite the staircase where we entered is a newly renovated "old" monastery, the **Dongak Chhyoling** Old Monastery. Below this and slightly further round is a small Hindu temple; as we have mentioned, Hinduism and Buddhism are closely intertwined in Nepal and nowhere more so than here. This temple is always so crowded with pilgrims that it is impossible for an outsider to get close to the main deity. The temple is dedicated

Sketch Map of Swayambhunath

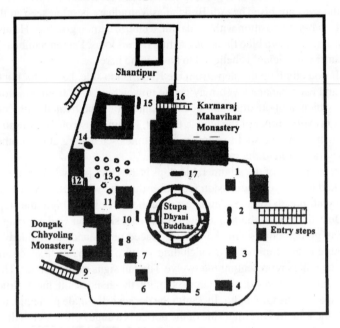

Key to Sketch Map of Swayambhunath

1	Pratapur shikhara temple	9	Museum
2	Dorjee/vajra	10	Taras
3	Anantapur shikhara temple	11	Ajima/Harati temple
4	Vasupur temple/Vasundhara	12	Ashokan bodhisattva
	Mandir	13	Chaityas and chortens
5	Shop and tmeple	14	Agnipur shrine
6	Vayupur temple	15	Akshobya Buddha
7	Five step stupa, Tashi Gorma	16	Café
	Chaitya	17	Nagapur shrine
8	Rajat Jainty egg		

Swayambhunath

primarily to **Ajima** (also called Harati), an ancient Newari mother goddess who is the deity of smallpox, a disease that tormented the valley until some years ago. Buddha appointed Ajima to protect the valley children. Ajima is considered by Buddhists to be Maya Devi, the mother of the Buddha. Today people come to offer homage and give grain, yoghurt and incense etc. to the black idol of the temple. The Tara deities are seen here as bronze images.

On the northwest side are many chaityas and a shrine to **Agni,** the Vedic god of fire. Further around is a strange pit with a slug-like image. This is the **Nagapur,** a place to pay homage to the snake naga spirits and pray for rain. Continuing round, we come to the delightful Tibetan **Karmaraj Mahavihar** monastery. Just inside the entrance sits an imposing vision of Buddha Shakyamuni. In here you can sit and while away the hours listening to the evocative, hypnotic chants and drums of the monks. Dream away the troubles of this earth, float away into another world...

One time around the stupa is of course not enough. On your second circuit you may note the nine Buddha figures carefully caged away in niches within the stupa, behind two sets of iron bars. Peering in through the bars you will see exquisitely painted figures cloaked in fine silks. Those at the cardinal points are four of the five **Dhyani Buddhas** who represent the fundamental elements of fire, water, air and earth. The fifth, near the entrance, represents space (ether). The other four are the tantric female aspects that represent wisdom. The male and female aspects must unite for enlightenment. The torana, the gold plaques above the all-seeing eyes, also show the five Dhyani Buddhas, collectively known as the panchabuddhas. Above this thirteen golden steps represent the thirteen steps to enlightenment, capped by the summit crown, which is said to contain precious jewels.

Continuing now past the Hindu temple and straight past the large group of small chaityas, we go down the hill. Here is the **Shantipur** building or Mansion of Peace, which is not often open. This mystical tantric complex is said to be the home of an 8th century tantric, Shantikar Acharya, who, it is said, is still in a meditative trance deep in an underground chamber. A fascinating story tells how King Pratap Malla went down into the depths of the temple in 1658, fighting off demons and serpents in order to bring out into the light an ancient mandala. When he did this, longed-for rain fell in the valley and abundant crops ensued. This sacred site has on the walls inside the first chamber some colourful frescoes, depicting the legends of Swayambhu. You can see these frescoes from the door as you peer in.

Of course around this stupa there are also many small shops selling Buddhist singing bowls, prayer wheels and other memorabilia. There is also a small museum displaying sculptures and another stupa down the steps to the west. (Taxis are found here as well). A couple of cafés offer snacks and refreshments while you enjoy the stunning view, before the journey back to the city.

Swayambhu is perched high on a hilltop, and the base of this hill has now been surrounded by finely painted stupas and a **new prayer wall**, with hundreds of prayer wheels waiting to be turned to send prayers heavenwards; prayers for eternal peace which so desperately need to be answered. On the western area is a new but very imposing **golden Buddha**. It is 57 feet high. Also here in the **Buddha Amideva** park are a couple of impressive stupas and a vision of **Milarepa's cave**, with the poet inside and a conch shell by the opening, which local people blow to awaken the hard-of-hearing poet within. A multi-coloured stupa just to the north houses an enormous prayer wheel and some amazing new paintings and images. A thousand-armed eleven-headed vision of **Avalokiteshvara** is prominent, with a Mahakala face as one of the top faces.

There is a very pleasant walk around the base of the hill on the north side to the main Kathmandu side entrance. Before the eastern gate are many large stupas. One has another gigantic prayer wheel and images of Tibetan saints, gurus and the different Buddha figures of the Tibetan sects. The different large stupas represent the different stages of Buddha's life. A large colourful statue of **Padma Sambhava** sits on his lotus plinth. He holds the trident, a dorjee and a vessel.

Swayambhunath is the beginning of time, the Adi Buddha, the self-created, self-existent one. And this Buddha, with curious mysterious eyes, still resides on the hill that grew from the lotus plant out of a vast lake.

Kathmandu is the valley of the Buddha, the valley of the Gods and Goddesses, where legend, myth and reality merge in a cacophony of chaotic disorder. Where the green-eyed yellow idol, that missing mysterious god who sees all, is but is unseen.

Dorjee/Vajra

217

CHAPTER TWELVE
The End of the Road

Our senses have been overpowered by the myriad of colour, exotica, erotica and sublime imagery. We have found those seemingly lost scenes of enchantment. The visual onslaught of the temples, shrines and stupas leaves vivid images in our minds. The overwhelming vitality of the people, their culture and their festivities leaves imprints on our subconscious. Our magical journey into the mists of time around the valley is at an end. The mountains beckon — the home of the gods.

The Rum Doodle New Year 2000

Rum Doodle is a mountain in a faraway land, deep in the Himalayas. Its icy summit is 40,000 and a half feet high. Only mad dogs and Englishmen seek to tame its vicious faces. Even the dogs have decided not to embark on its sheer buttresses.

In a corner of Thamel is a restaurant and bar that captures the spirit of this mystical mountain, where only large feet may tread. Now Rum Doodle has more big feet on its vertical walls than the number of porters needed for the ascent of the mystical rum-looking peak itself. Its location is sometimes a mystery. It too moves quickly and quietly from one lane to another. For over twenty years Rum Doodle has been reincarnated in different parts of Thamel, but its dedicated devotees will always seek it out.

Arriving overland with our group of oldies in December 1999, it was inevitable that the new millennium would have to be celebrated in the charming domain of this god of misty mountains. For the reincarnate deity of Rum Doodle is a Rinpoche, a guru and deity who looks after food and booze. But Rum Doodle has no earthly form, for it is a fiction of a writer's vivid imagination.

Rum Doodle

Everest, the Fiftieth Anniversary!

In May 2003 celebrations to mark the fiftieth anniversary of the first ascent of Mount Everest were held throughout the valley. Patan Durbar Square held a reception for the summit climbers amid celebrations of Rato Machhendranath and a Hindu mela. On May 27th Sir Edmund and Lady Hillary, Junko Tabei, Reinhold Messner, Tashi and Jamling Tenzing were among those riding the streets of Kathmandu in horse-drawn carriages.

The Rum Doodle restaurant paid homage to the fiftieth anniversary celebrations of Everest with a special dinner for many of the 'summiteers'. Among the honoured guests were M. S. Kohli, the first Indian summiteer, and Junko Tabei, the first woman to summit in May 1975. (The vast Japanese women's expedition carried masses of equipment including ladders, which Bob witnessed going up from Lukla to Namche in March 1975.)

The festivities concluded on May 29th with a Gala Dinner for Sir Edmund Hillary at the Hyatt Hotel in Boudhanath. Many Sherpas and Sherpanis were flown down from the Khumbu to join Sir Edmund and Lady Hillary at the party. Two animated dancing yaks enlivened the celebrations. Dancing and music enthralled the crowd, and a band of bagpipers heralded the arrival of the Scottish whisky dignitaries, who gave a generous donation to the Himalayan Trust as well as a 50-year-old bottle of finest Scotch to Sir Edmund! The evening concluded with a traditional Sherpa dance, and a jolly good time was had by all.

The Last Word... for now...

In our early visits here we were mainly concerned with the mountains, the Himalaya, the spiritual abode of the gods, although that aspect did not seem so obvious on the first visit of youth. Trekking among the highest mountains of the world has its own special magic; we have not yet found the yeti, but there is certainly a sense of some all-pervading higher power.

Now that we are doing less trekking, we have come to spend more and more time in the valley itself, never ceasing to be surprised at what it has to offer. As time has passed, we have come back year after year, and every time without fail we have found new corners of the city just waiting to be discovered. With more time to study and absorb the ancient cultures, which are still so alive today, we have learnt so much more about life here. The answers are never clear, but it is an indescribable pleasure to sit on a rooftop at Boudhanath on a Saturday, listening to the spellbinding music, smelling the enchanting juniper and incense, absorbing the magical atmosphere and just gazing at the distant Himalayan peaks, the abode of the gods.

Nepal is indeed a land of peace, tranquillity and beauty. It has wonderful mountains for trekkers and mountaineers, it has exquisite art forms and it has exciting white water and wildlife in the Chitwan National Park to the south of the country.

In short, it has something for everyone, and we hope that this guide will have given you some ideas, as well as being a practical guide to some of the exotic and erotic places to visit in the Kathmandu Valley.

(K.C. - is it Kaput Crazy or Khatri Chhetri!!)

221

Historical Dates

Licchavi Period	350 to 740 AD. approx.
Abhira Gupta	506 to 641
King Manadeva	464 to 505
King Narendradeva	643 to 679
Lost Period	740 to 1200
Anandadeva	1147 to 1166
Early Mallas	1200 to 1482
Ari Malla	1200 to 1216
Ananta Malla	1274 to 1308
Sthitiraja Malla	1382 to 1395
Yaksha Malla	1428 to 1482 approx.

Golden Malla Period   **1482 to 1769**

Kathmandu

Jaya Ratna Malla	1484 to 1520
Mahendra Malla	1562 to 1574
Shivasimha Malla	1574 to 1581
Pratap Malla	1641 to 1674
Jayaprakash Malla	1735 to 1768

Patan

Siddhi Narasingha Malla	1619 to 1661
Shrinivasa Malla	1661 to 1684
Yoganendra Malla	1684 to 1705

Bhaktapur

Jagatjyoti Malla	1613 to 1637
Jitamitra Malla	1673 to 1696
Bhupatindra Malla	1696 to 1722
Ranajita Malla	1722 to 1769

The Shah Kings

Prithvi Narayan Shah	1768/9 to 1775
Rajendra Bikram	1816 to 1847

Other kings followed, but had no power under the Ranas.

The Ranas   **1846 to 1950/1**

Return of the Shah Kings
Tribhuvan	1951 to 1955
Mahendra	1955 to 1972
Birendra	1972 to 2001
Dipendra	June 1 - 3, 2001
Gyanendra	June 3, 2001 -

King Gyanendra is the 13th Shah king to have ruled Nepal since the Shah dynasty began.

Don't Pass Out!

The Green Eye of the Yellow God

There's a one-eyed yellow idol to the north of Kathmandu,
There's a little marble cross below the town;
There's a broken-hearted woman tends the grave of Mad Carew,
And the Yellow God forever gazes down.

He was known as "Mad Carew" by the subs of Kathmandu,
He was better than they felt inclined to tell;
But for all his foolish pranks, he was worshipped in the ranks,
And the Colonel's daughter smiled on him as well.

He had loved her all along, with the passion of the strong,
The fact that she loved him was plain to all.
She was nearly twenty-one and arrangements had begun
To celebrate her birthday with a ball.

He wrote to ask what present she would like from Mad Carew,
They met next day, as he dismissed a squad;
And jestingly she told him then that nothing else would do
But the green eye of the little Yellow God.

On the night before the dance, Mad Carew seemed in a trance,
And they chaffed him as they puffed at their cigars;
But for once he failed to smile, and he sat alone awhile,
Then went out into the night beneath the stars.

He returned before the dawn, with his shirt and tunic torn,
And a gash across his temples dripping red;
He was patched up right away, and he slept all through the day,
And the Colonel's daughter watched beside his bed.

He woke at last and asked if they could send his tunic through;
She brought it and he thanked her with a nod;
He bade her search the pocket, saying, "That's from Mad Carew,"
And she found the little green eye of the god.

She upbraided poor Carew in the way that women do,
Thought both her eyes were strangely hot and wet;
But she wouldn't take the stone, and Carew was left alone,
With the jewel that he'd chanced his life to get.

When the ball was at its height, on that still and tropic night,
She thought of him and hastened to his room;
As she crossed the barrack square, she could hear the dreamy
air

Of a waltz tune softly stealing through the gloom.

His door was open wide, with silver moonlight shining through,
The place was wet and slipp'ry where she trod;
An ugly knife lay buried in the heart of Mad Carew,
'Twas the "Vengeance of the little Yellow God."

There's a one-eyed yellow idol to the north of Kathmandu,
There's a little marble cross below the town;
There's a broken-hearted woman tends the grave of Mad Carew,
And the Yellow God forever gazes down.

J. Milton Hayes

Related Topics and Books by Pilgrims

Pilgrims Publications has recently devoted a lot of time and energy to presenting new books on the subject of spiritual growth by meditation, yoga, Tantra, religious paths and erotic art forms. Earlier related publications and topics are also listed below.

Erotic Art of the Kathmandu Valley by Bob Gibbons and Siân Pritchard-Jones
Introduction to the Kama Sutra by Bob Gibbons and Siân Pritchard-Jones *Introduction to Tantra and Erotic Practice* by Bob Gibbons and Siân Pritchard-Jones

Memoirs of Jail by Siddhi Charan Shrestha
Princess Bhrikuti Devi by Min Bahadur Sakya
Faith Healers of the Himalaya by Casper Miller
Nepalese Casted Vessels, Decanters and Bowls by Matthew S. Friedman
Manifestations of Shiva by Stella Karmisch
Nepalese Festivals by Jim Goodman
Tantric Healing in the Kathmandu Valley by Angela Dietrich

Earlier Publications

Kriya Yoga by Jo Santiago
Sacred Symbols of Hinduism by Jo Santiago
Sacred Symbols of Buddhism by Jo Santiago

Other Titles used as Reference

Festivals of Nepal by Mary E. Anderson
The Iconography of Tibetan Lamaism by Antoinette Gordon
The Iconography of Nepalese Buddhism by Min Bahadur Shakya
My Kind of Kathmandu by Desmond Doig
Power Places of Kathmandu by Dowman and Bubriski
Nepal Valley of the Gods by Held and Beguin
The Kathmandu Valley by John Sanday
Patan Museum Transformation of a Royal Palace of Nepal by Gotz Hagmuller.
Tibetan Paintings by George Roerich

MORE TITLES ON MOUNTAINEERING AND TREKKING FROM PILGRIMS PUBLISHING

- **Among the Himalayas** .... *L A Waddel*
- **Annapurna South Face** .... *Chris Bonington*
- **Attack on Everest** .... *Hugh Ruttledge*
- **Climbing the Fish Tail** .... *Wilfred Noyce*
- **Everest:** From the first attempt to the final victory. .... *Micheline Morin*
- **Everest the Challenge** .... *Sir Francis Younghusband*
- **Everest: the Hard Way**
  (The adventure story of the Decade) .... *Chris Bonington*
- **First Over Everest:** The Huston-Mount Everest Expedition 1933
  .... *P F M Fellowes, L V Stewart Blacker, P T Etherton & others*
- **Himalayan Adventure Trekking Gear:**
  A Checklist for Women .... *Joyce A Tapper*
- **Lost in the Himalayas** .... *James Scott & Joanne Robertson*
- **Manaslu: A Trekker's Guide** .... *Kev Reynolds*
- **Man of Everest:** *The Autobiography of Tenzing* .... *J R Ullman*
- **Mount Everest 1938** .... *H W Tilman*
- **Mount Everest :** The Reconnaissance 1921 .... *C K Howard-Bury*
- **Mustang: A Trekking Guide** .... *Bob Gibbons and Siân Pritchard-Jones*
- **Mustang: Un Guide de Trekking** ... .*Bob Gibbons and Siân Pritchard-Jones*
- **Nepal Die Far Western Region:**
  Reisecompanion für Abenteurer, Trekker und Bergsteiger .... *M Lindenfelser*
- **Nepal Himalaya** .... *H W Tilman*
- **Nepal the Far Western Region:** A Travelling
  Companion for Travellers, Trekkers and Climbers .... *M Lindenfelser*
- **Peaks and Lamas** .... *Marco Pallis*
- **Round Kangchenjunga** .... *Douglas W Freshfield*
- **The Assault on Mount Everest 1922** .... *C G Bruce*
- **The Epic of Mount Everest** .... *Sir Francis Younghusband*
- **The Fight for Everest 1924** .... *E F Norton*

www.pilgrimsbooks.com

For Catalog and more Information Mail or Fax to:

PILGRIMS BOOK HOUSE

Mail Order, P. O. Box 3872, Kathmandu, Nepal
Tel: 977-1-4700919 Fax: 977-1-4700943
E-mail: mailorder@pilgrims.wlink.com.np